Here is the deeply inspirational and exciting story of World Vision, one of America's most vital missionary organizations, and of its dedicated and restless founder, Dr. Bob Pierce, who reflects the true missionary spirit in his constant prayer: "Let my heart be broken with the things that break the heart of God."

Written by a thoroughly practical but perceptive observer who is not a member of World Vision, *Let My Heart Be Broken* records in moving detail the stirring accomplishments and sacrifices of missionary heroes who operate hospitals, clinics, schools, and missions throughout the world today.

Richard Gehman accompanied Bob Pierce on a global tour, and this book tells how, through the work of a tireless little American woman in the World Vision organization, pathetic lepers in Formosa find new purpose in life; how Communist infiltrators have marked every Hong Kong missionary for death when the Reds take the city; how manacled war criminals in Japan marched to their execution singing hymns after their lives had been touched by a colorful British woman missionary known as "Sensei"; and how devoted doctors and nurses, teachers and preachers venture with faith alone into places of disease and great danger.

Traveling with Mr. Gehman was Richard Reinhold, a gifted photographer, who has captured the drama and inspiration of World Vision's magnificent in the midst of suffering, hope.

n is really two unt of the tirerking under Bob ce, and—between the lines—an own unfolding awareness of what these people do, and why they do it.

LET MY HEART
BE BROKEN...

with the things

that break the heart of GOD

Richard Gehman

Photographs by Richard Reinhold

McGraw-Hill Book Company, Inc.
New York   Toronto   London

LET MY HEART BE BROKEN

To Dr. Bob Pierce
who showed us his way

NOTE

Early in 1959, Dr. Robert Willard Pierce, better known as "Dr. Bob," founder and president of World Vision, Inc., invited me to fly across the Pacific and visit some of the orphanages, missions, hospitals, leprosariums, and sanitariums, as well as pastors' conferences, churches, and Bible schools, supported wholly or in part by that organization. He felt that it was time that the work of these devout and dedicated people be brought to the attention of the general public by an unbiased outsider. With Richard Reinhold, a photographer and old friend, I traveled over 30,000 miles. Dr. Bob introduced me to scores of people who have given their lives to the service of God; we lived with them, watched them at work, saw what they had accomplished and heard them tell what they hope to accomplish. As the trip progressed and I became more and more affected by what I saw, it became clear that this had to be more than a job of storytelling. I therefore cast the book in the form of a journal, interrupting the entries from time to time to tell about people I met. I did this because I could not write the book without trying to communicate the deep impact these people had upon my own life.

R. G.

CONTENTS

The foolishness of God is wiser than men; and the weakness of God is stronger than men. For ye see your calling, brethren, how that not many wise men after the flesh, not many mighty, not many noble, are called: But God hath chosen the foolish things of the world to confound the wise; and God hath chosen the weak things of the world to confound the things which are mighty. . . .

—From the First Epistle of Paul
the Apostle to the Corinthians

LET MY HEART BE BROKEN

We have come more than 7000 miles, but our real journey has not yet begun. My friend Richard Reinhold, the photographer, and I are flying out to the Far East with Dr. Bob Pierce, president of World Vision, Inc., of Pasadena, California, to see the work being done by the people and institutions World Vision helps to support. Reinhold and I flew from New York to Los Angeles to Honolulu, where Bob Pierce was waiting for us at the airport, a tall, robust man with a white shock of curly hair topping his figure, a battered brown satchel in one hand, and an overcoat in a plastic bag thrown over his arm. As we were waiting to board the aircraft for Tokyo, Bob glanced at the name on its side and said, " 'City of Kyoto'—I've flown on her before. She's a DC-6, not very fast, but she's a good ship." He walked up the stairs as unconcernedly as a man boarding a commuter train. Reinhold and I were breathless with neck-craning, eye-straining excitement, for this is our first trip to Japan—but to Bob, this was only another step in the long journey to which he has dedicated his life. During the past ten years he has logged an average of 200,000 flying miles per year. As soon as he was on board the "City of Kyoto" he stowed his overcoat in the rack above the seat, put his brown bag under it, sat down, pulled down the knot of his necktie and opened his collar, fastened his safety belt, bowed his head for several minutes in prayer, then leaned back and fell asleep. The ritual was all the more remarkable because it was so automatic. . . .

Now we have been airborne for two or three hours. The

flight is smooth but we are bucking 8o-mph head winds, and they add to the effect of suspension ordinarily experienced by passengers flying in a clear sky over a smooth, rippleless ocean. This stillness, felt against the soothing brocades with which the comfort-conscious Japan Air Lines has fitted out the cabin, has sent most of my fellow American passengers into sprawling sleep in abandoned postures. The Japanese passengers, on the other hand, seem unwilling or unable to lose their natural sense of order and design; even though they too are relaxed, their bodies are symmetrical and look as though they were carefully posed.

Across the aisle from me, Bob Pierce has awakened and is reading a book. Bob is—in his words—"an evangelistic minister." His primary concern is, as he says, leading people to Christ. Yet he also is world-minded; that is why he founded World Vision. Now Bob's gray-white hair is tossed in cowlicks and stray strands, and the collar of his light blue pullover shirt is turned up rebelliously. As he reads, he frowns—not in disapproval but in concentration. I do not know Bob at all well; I met him only a few months ago; but in the short space of our acquaintance I have learned that he cannot conceal his true emotions. He seems to me to be one of the few naturally, uncontrollably honest men I have ever met; his prevailing temper is one of enthusiasm and zest for life, but when he is troubled, he is troubled to the depths of his soul. When that happens, he prays, and more often than not, he prays aloud, wherever he is, in the middle of whatever he is doing. Soon after we first met in New York, I took him to dinner at The Colony, a place where displays of any kind are frowned upon. Bob said grace before dinner, aloud, and everybody at our table bowed his head along with him. I don't suppose anybody ever said grace in The Colony before.

The book Bob is reading is *The Ugly American,* by William J. Lederer and Eugene Burdick. That it is disturbing him is apparent from the tight compression of his lips and the lines on his forehead. Presently he realizes that I have been staring at him. "Pretty good book here," he says. "You ought to read it—we'll be visiting some of the places these stories are set in.

"There's one thing about the book that disturbs me, though," Bob continues. "In the whole book, the writers mention only one missionary—a Roman Catholic priest. It looks to me as though they aren't aware that missionaries in the Far East, all over the map, are doing the very kind of thing they think the government should do. These writers say that instead of building huge dams, bridges, power plants, factories, and so on—instead of doing that to fight communism, we ought to be going in and helping the poor people, the sick and the distressed, the ones too ignorant to help themselves . . . and that we ought to go in and help them on their own level, in ways they can understand.

"These writers don't seem to realize that missionaries are doing just that *all the time,* and have been for over three hundred years. When we get to some of the places we're going, you'll see these things with your own eyes. Wait'll you meet Lil Dickson . . . the Moffetts . . . and the rest. I can't even begin to list them all. You'll see. The trouble is, many people have little real knowledge of what missionaries actually do.

"These two men have the right idea," Bob says, tapping the book, "but they don't go far enough. They should have gone up into some of the far places—into Assam and Nepal, into the mountain regions of Formosa, where the tribes were head-hunters only a generation ago. Then they would have realized that not all Americans are lying down on the job. The missionaries aren't. You'll see."

He picks up the book again. From time to time he takes out his pen and underlines a passage, biting his lip.

To some degree I am skeptical of what Bob Pierce says. I have come on this trip not because I am a religious person—I am not—but because I am convinced that Bob will lead me to important and meaningful material, and because I always have been attracted to people who are committed, whose convictions are strong, and whose energy is arresting. Before we started, I made clear to Bob that it would be difficult for him to convince me of the reality of his vision, his sense of the living presence of Christ.

"I'm not going to argue with you, buddy," he said. "All I want you to do is see for yourself—and if you are impressed by what you see, if you think others should know about it, I pray God you'll write about it." That is a fair enough arrangement, and as I now consider it, on this first leg of our long journey, I wonder if perhaps I entered into it because, like so many people, I am looking for something in which I can believe.

We stop at Wake for breakfast and are off again. Our first sight of the islands of Japan comes around 6 P.M., Tokyo time. The setting sun is hidden by fat purple clouds; its rays fan out downward into the green-blue sea and over the brown patches of earth, like some stylized design on a Japanese fan. Small boats with flimsy sails put in and out from the tiny islands. I half expect to hear someone strike a soft, resounding gong behind my ear.

At the airport, we are rushed through customs more quickly than I ever have experienced it before. The desk clerks and bellboys at the New Imperial are as polite and efficient as the customs clerks were, and in five minutes we are in our rooms, which have a connecting door between. No sooner are we in than Bob's telephone rings.

"Hello, Joe!" he cries. "How are you, buddy? Yes, yes, fine flight. Just this minute got in. How're you, anyhow? Tell me all about it, Joe."

The caller is the Reverend Joe R. Gooden, a minister who has taken a leave of absence from his regular work to make preliminary arrangements for the huge Osaka Evangelistic Crusade which World Vision is planning to conduct in the spring. Previously, Bob had explained to me that this year marks the hundredth anniversary of the coming of Protestant missionaries to Japan. The country always has resisted Christianity—which is odd, considering its willingness to adopt Western customs and beliefs in secular areas. The ministers of the various denominations always have found their work hard going, and many have been so busy with their own problems they have not had the time or inclination to unite with their fellows. Now Bob and his workers in World Vision are endeavoring to get many of the churches in the huge Osaka area to cooperate in one huge evangelistic campaign. Joe Gooden is the "advance man." Later, we are to learn more of what he has been doing out here.

"Joe's got a big job," Bob says, after he puts down the telephone. "We're not sure we can bring it off. Nobody's ever managed to get all these churches to cooperate yet, but we're praying God will help us do it this time. If the Lord blesses us, it could be one of the biggest things for the Protestant church that ever happened in Japan."

After washing up, we go out to a sukiyaki place to eat. The Mama-San remembers Bob well, and hastens to seat us on the floor at a low table. The food is superb: onion slices, mushrooms, scallions, chunks of bean curd, a spinachlike vegetable, another curious green vegetable that to my astonishment turns out to be edible chrysanthemum, and strips of lean, beautifully marbled beef, all cooked together at the table in an iron skillet greased with suet and *shoju* sauce. As we eat, Bob resumes the conversation we had begun on the aircraft:

"As I was saying when I was reading that book, some people in the State Department and the U.S. Information Service don't seem to recognize the impact and significance of the work the missionaries are doing. The Defense Department won't even give missionaries Post Exchange permits on army bases. They have to get along on what they're paid by their churches, and in most places they have to pay full prices for everything they buy—whereas military and political personnel get reductions. The shame of it is, there are missionaries I know of who have to get along on a hundred dollars, and less, a month. Yet they go on, serving not only God but their country as well. And still the country refuses to give some of them recognition.

"What's even more alarming to me is that even some missionaries' *churches* don't support them the way they should. Every time I come out here, I see new areas of need—places where missionaries are struggling along on practically nothing. That's where World Vision comes in. We don't *start* any projects. We go and survey a situation, and if help is needed, we try to see that whoever needs it, gets it. The trouble is, there's so much to do. I often feel like we're never doing enough."

I remark that it seems to me that people in the United States ought to be made aware, somehow, of the needs.

"Yes, they should," Bob says. "That's what I hope you'll do. Everywhere you'll go on this trip, you'll find stories—not necessarily stories of great heroism, or sacrifice, but stories of people doing day-to-day jobs that really might not seem like much, but which are great and genuine services to Jesus Christ. That's the kind of thing I hope you'll write about. Oh, there are so many of them! I could sit for hours and tell you about them, but I want you to see them for yourself. Right here in Tokyo, for example, there's a little old lady I want you to meet, one of the most remarkable women I ever met in my life. Her name is Irene Webster-Smith. They call her Sensei."

§ "AS THOU GOEST, STEP BY STEP . . ."

Irene Webster-Smith came in to see us for a hasty breakfast in the hotel that first morning in Tokyo. I watched her while she chattered away to Bob Pierce, telling of her activities. It was hard for me, at first, to find out what was so remarkable about her, or why World Vision should be supporting her work, as it does from time to time. Later, when I got to know her better, I found out the reasons. But at breakfast she seemed just another missionary. She is a short, cheerful, bustling, gray-haired woman whose eyes gleam behind her spectacles like those of a wise little bird. She lives in a single room in a student center she organized and built almost singlehandedly in the crowded university section of Tokyo. The students who go there all call her *Sensei*, which means "teacher" or "wise one." They know her as a woman of great warmth, sympathy, and deep faith. Some of them believe she is a lonely woman who has found satisfaction in her work. Actually, she is far from lonely. She is too busy to know an instant of loneliness. She is intensely happy in the service she has chosen—a service so important to her that, by dedicating herself to it, she lost the chance for a happy and contented married life in her waning years. But that is only part of what makes her remarkable.

Sensei does not like to talk about herself, I learned. She does not even talk much about the work she is doing. Many religious leaders who have visited her student center declare that she is doing as much, and perhaps more, to convert the youth of Japan to Christianity than any other individual, but to hear her talk about the student activities, she is hardly making a contribution at all. "We just hold a few services and some Bible classes," she says deprecatingly. She does not mention the hundreds of young men and women she personally has led to Christ, nor the hundreds they in turn have led. Nor does she tell the story of how General Douglas MacArthur, when he assumed his duties as Supreme Allied Commander and determined to send out a call for former missionaries to Japan who could assist him in his work, heard of her previous career in Japan and demanded that she be the first missionary called back. When such things are mentioned to Sensei, she says, "Oh, I'm not certain at all that that's true." And she changes the subject.

Sensei's story began, she told me, when she was a teen-ager. Born in Wales more than sixty years ago, she was taken to Dublin by her mother to live when she was about three, after the death of her father. In Ireland, her mother, who was a Friend, then married a man named Duffy, a Roman Catholic. Duffy let his stepchildren follow their mother's faith; he insisted only that they get a good education in Greek and Latin and music.

"When I was a little person I felt I loved the Lord, but only

as a little person would," says Sensei in her soft Irish accent. "I
couldn't really say that I'd ever had a personal transaction.
Well, when I was in my teens one of my brothers picked up
the *Irish Times* one day and saw that a boy named Fritz Wood,
who'd been a neighbor of ours, was going to speak. They
called him The Boy Preacher. I believe he was seventeen. He
was preaching in a slum-quarter meetinghouse. We decided
to go to hear him. Now, on this special night I was wearing a
lovely brown dress and a brown velvet hat and coat. I enjoyed the singing, and I enjoyed hearing the Wood boy speaking. For some time I had been thinking that I ought to make
some sort of personal decision, but I just had not done it. After
the meeting, the Wood boy and his family asked some of us
to stay. I felt conspicuous, because I had a feather on my hat.
A lady said to me, 'Are you saved?' and before I could answer, she looked at the feather and added, 'I can see that
you're not.' I began to go, but at the door another lady welcomed me back. One of Fritz Wood's brothers then asked
me to come back, too, but I was still a bit miffed. I did not
stay. But that night I got to thinking about what they had
asked in the meeting—'Do you know Christ as your own personal friend?' I had a Bible with a concordance. I looked up
Saviour and *Friend* because I wanted to see what He could
mean to me. And then I simply asked Him to be my Saviour
and Friend. The next morning, at the time when I ordinarily
practiced the piano, my stepfather came in and asked me what
I was playing. 'That doesn't sound like Czerny to me,' he said.
I said, 'Oh, it's just a chorus of a hymn,' and I told him and my
mother about the wonderful experience I'd had. Mother said,
'We're very happy for you, but you needn't talk so much
about it.' "

The young girl graduated from Kildare College in Dublin, where she received a standard academic education that also permitted her courses in shorthand, typing, and business law. Soon afterward she won a job in Dublin Castle with the Solicitor General. For a time she had some thought of continuing her studies in law, but then she read an article in a magazine telling about an organization in Japan called the Japan Evangelistic Band. Barclay Buxton, an English Episcopalian minister, had gone to Japan in 1900 or thereabouts and presently had been joined by a man named Padgett-Wilkes. Together they had formed the group. They needed assistance badly. The article changed Irene Webster-Smith's life.

"They were trying to rescue young girls who were being sold as geisha," she recalls. "They told about a Miss Penrod, from Arkansas, who was helping them in the work. It seemed like a real call to me. I said to my mother, 'I feel that God wants me in Japan.' She said, 'Nonsense, child.' But the next morning she apologized and said, 'You'll go to Japan, but not until I'm Home.' She meant Heaven, of course."

That was in 1915. In August, her mother died of cancer. Almost at once she went to Edinburgh, Scotland, and enrolled in the Faith Mission Bible College, where she not only studied but helped conduct a mission for street urchins. "They came ragged to us and without shoes," she recalls, "and we had baths for them, and bound up their wounds, and helped them buy boots. We held a Sunday school, and worked among girls who sold fruits and vegetables. We helped the sick and tried to soothe domestic difficulties. Oh, there was plenty to do in the slums of Edinburgh! But my mind was still on Japan. It was as though He was insisting that I go out there. I stayed at the Faith Mission about six months, and then applied to go. Strangely enough, I was the only person who answered the appeal they had made in the magazine."

On October 9, 1916, she sailed for Japan. Because it was wartime, the ship took a circuitous route and did not arrive until December 23. The girl put the time to good use: "I helped the officers and men with English lessons, and they tried to teach me Japanese. I arrived in Japan with quite a vocabulary—but the trouble was, it was men's Japanese, and I had to unlearn a lot of it."

In Japan she went to live with the family of George Braithwaite, an Englishman who was a missionary and translator, founder of the Japan Book and Tract Society, in order to learn the language. Mrs. Braithwaite became ill, and the girl took over the housekeeping chores. This sent her out into the markets to buy provisions, and the regular contact with the tradespeople helped her learn the language quickly. Today, Sensei speaks Japanese as well as she speaks English.

Once each week, she went to the rescue home conducted by Miss Christine Penrod to help her with correspondence. Miss Penrod's home was the only one of its kind in Japan. At that time, vice was common throughout the country. Brothelkeepers would go to poor farmers with many children and persuade them to give up their daughters, promising to educate them and give them good homes and eventually find them husbands. Miss Penrod provided a haven for such girls; when they ran away from the brothels, she took them in and hid them, not only from their owners but also from the police. After a few months, Sensei moved in with Miss Penrod as a full-time assistant.

Life in the rescue home was not without its excitement. "One day," Sensei recalls, "I came home from shopping to find a lot of rough-looking men and police there. They had come to look for a girl who had run away from one of their houses. I knew the girl—she was with us, all right. But I pretended I didn't understand what they wanted. I just walked up the path to our main house. We had a cook, then, who had twin boys, and I found them playing with my parasol. I stopped to talk to them. One of the policemen came up and grabbed me by the shoulder and said, 'Do you think we have nothing to do but wait while you play with children? We are going to search the house!' I said nothing, but went right up to the house and took off my shoes, preparatory to going in. He forged ahead of me and threw open the door and went into the house without taking off his shoes. Then he came back to me and grabbed me by the shoulders again and said, 'Where is she?' I pointed to a room where I thought the girl was. He pulled open that door and looked into the room. There was a window there, half open. 'She's escaped,' I said to him. He became furious. He was so furious he took me and threw me down the stairs. Then he ran out of the house. I was only a bit shaken up—but not so much that I couldn't laugh at him. He'd run right past the girl. The other girls had disguised her as an old lady, and she'd been there all the time."

The girls in the home did not take readily to Christian teachings, which further complicated the two ladies' work. "They professed Christianity," Sensei says, "but they often backslid. One morning I became so disgusted I said to Miss Penrod, 'It would be nice if we had a little earthquake that would shake some of these girls into Heaven.' "

Instead of an earthquake, there was an epidemic of influenza in 1918. Usually there were about eighty girls in the home. Out of that number, fifty died. "I did nothing but go from deathbed to deathbed for days," she says. "Miss Penrod herself got the disease, and I was without help for a long time. Then a helper from the Evangelistic Band arrived, and together we laid out the dead in rough wooden boxes. We tried to give them decent burials, but there was not much we could do."

By the time the epidemic was over, Sensei had all but decided that she had had enough of Japan. For one thing, she originally had planned to stay only a year or two. More important, there was a young man waiting for her. Before going to Japan, she had promised this young man, a minister whom she refers to today only as Al, that she would marry him as soon as she came back from her call. On the boat back from Japan, she became even more determined not to return. It was a rat-infested craft, jammed with refugees from all over the Orient, and the voyage was a horrible one. Yet something about the filth and the misery of the refugees affected her profoundly. "I thought: God gave me this work—it is my burden," she says. A voice inside her answered, "There isn't anything that can be done to save those girls." And then another voice said, "We should put a fence at the top of the precipice rather than an ambulance at the bottom." That made up her mind. She would return to Japan and start a home that would take in girls before they could fall into the hands of the brothelkeepers.

The ship docked at Vancouver. She stayed for a few days with some missionaries. In their house she saw a framed motto, a verse from Proverbs: "As thou goest, step by step, I will open up the way before thee."

It gave her hope. She was certain that her decision was the right one. In New York, on her way back to Dublin, she read biographies of two missionaries who had devoted their lives to helping orphans, Hudson Taylor and George Mueller. "Their lives made a great impression on me," she says, "because they trusted in God to help them." Just before she boarded the boat for England, a woman asked her what she planned to do. She told of her dream. Impulsively, the woman pressed a twenty-dollar bill into her hand. She felt that that was a sign.

In London she went to see the Japan Evangelistic Band and told the leaders of her plan to save orphan girls. Barclay Buxton, the founder, said, "I feel God has given you a mission and a faith to carry it out." But the Band could not help her because its mission was primarily evangelistic. "However, we will stand behind you and pray for you," Buxton said.

The thought that she would be on her own did not deter her for an instant. She went home to Dublin to say good-by to her family before going back to Japan—and there found two more stumbling blocks. The first was her older brother, Will, who had been out in India as a surveyor until a native worker shot him in the stomach and he had had to come home to recuperate. Will had been engaged, but his intended bride suddenly had broken off the engagement. He wanted his sister to stay home and keep house for him. Then there was Al, the young minister to whom she herself was engaged.

"I felt I had to return his ring," she says. "And I did. He said he understood how I felt about Japan—he knew the Lord was calling me there. He said he would wait for me until my mission was completed. He gave me another ring on which was engraved, 'The Lord watch between me and thee while we are absent one from the other.' "

She set sail again for Japan. At Kobe, where she docked, she was met by Padgett-Wilkes of the Japan Evangelistic Band, who asked her to stay with his family and give him some help on a commentary on the Bible he was writing for translation into Japanese. When she told him about the orphanage she had in mind, he was immediately enthusiastic. One night at dinner he told some friends about it. Among them was a doctor who came from the south, near Kyoto.

"We have prayed for many years," said the doctor, whose name was Saiki, "for someone to do this kind of work. We have felt that no Japanese could do it—the Japanese are too close to the local customs."

Dr. Saiki went on to say that he was then building two houses in the country, in the Kyoto area. "You are welcome to use them," he said.

Sensei went down to see the houses soon afterward, but even though she thought they were ideally suited for her project, she demurred. "There was a stop in my mind," she says. "I asked God to make clear what I should do . . . and a kind of vibration said, 'Get thee down south.'"

She packed her few belongings and made the journey and moved into the house. As soon as she got there, she was terrified. "I prayed," she said, "and my first prayer was: 'Oh Lord, please don't send me anybody at first less than two years old.'"

The first child was scarcely a foot in length. It was a baby girl, three weeks old.

Dr. Saiki had sent a maternity nurse to help out, but on that first day the woman came down with a cold and had to go to bed. Sensei was left, to her horror, with the infant. She said, "When I looked at it, I prayed it wouldn't fall to bits if I touched it. I had nothing to put it in. Finally I fixed up a washtub with some blankets, and when I put it in there, it relaxed and stopped crying."

The mother of the baby was dying of cancer in Dr. Saiki's house. When she heard that a foreigner was taking care of her baby—"my dirty, diseased baby," she called it—she was astounded.

"Now I know what Dr. Saiki is talking about when he speaks of the love of God," she said. She was converted.

The baby itself lasted only a few weeks, then died as its mother had.

"I came back from the crematorium feeling very, very low," says Sensei, "only to find that there on my doorstep was a two-year-old."

After that, she got seven babies in rapid succession, all less than one year old. She had no money. She wrote to seven friends and said, "I'll take care of them, somehow, but you must pray for them." Today she says, "In 1939, I had twelve graduates from high school—and seven of them were the original seven."

Throughout the twenty-seven years she ran her haven, which she called the Sunrise Home, Sensei cared for eighty-seven children. She regarded each one as her own child. At one point, in the early days, Dr. Saiki went to her and, after a good deal of typical Japanese circumlocution, said, "You are making a mistake. You are loving these children too much."

"I tried to stop loving them," Sensei comments, "but I could not help the way I felt."

Support for the work came to her in various ways. Some, unexpectedly, came from the royal family of Japan. One day while she was in Tokyo a friend invited her to a garden party at the Emperor's palace. There some Japanese heard of her work and told the Emperor about it, and some of the people in the court contributed to the project. Sensei will not talk about this support; apparently the gifts were made with the understanding that they would remain a secret.

She had some unexpected setbacks, too. After a few years, Dr. Saiki could no longer help her, and she had to find a new place. She settled upon a house near Kobe, and moved into that. There, one night as she was returning home from marketing, a thief attacked her. He leaped out from behind a pole and slammed her up against a wall. The force of the blow caused the retina of her right eye to become detached.

As the years went on she kept up correspondence with her family and with Al. He had moved to America and had become pastor of a church in New Jersey. His letters indicated that he still was hopeful that someday they would be married. In 1939 she went home on furlough. In England, the authorities tried to persuade her not to return to Japan; they knew that there was likely to be trouble there. She ignored the warnings and returned, only to be met in Tokyo by the British ambassador, who said, "What brought you back? We're trying to get rid of people like you."

"My work brought me back," Sensei said. "My children."

By then she had moved the Sunrise Home to Akashi. The military police harassed her continually; they thought she was a spy of some kind. Yet she held on, determined to care for her children until they were old enough to go out into the world on their own. Her letters home never indicated any of the trouble she was having. Instead, they were full of funny stories and anecdotes. Her favorite one concerned the time she had gone to a mayor of a village looking for a new house.

"We are Buddhists here," he said. "We want no Christians."

"I'm not here as evangelist now," Sensei said. "I only want a place for my children."

"How many children have you got?"

"Twenty-four."

"Twenty-four? How many husbands have you had?"

She also liked to tell about one house she moved into, which was said to be haunted. A doctor had been performing abortions in it, and all the townspeople were persuaded that the spirits of the patients who had died still haunted the rooms. "We just went from room to room and prayed, and the children weren't frightened any more," Sensei says.

By November 1940, with English and American citizens leaving Japan in droves, she finally decided that it was time for her to depart. She announced her decision to the congregation at her regular Sunday meeting, and asked them to care for her children. At the time, she had forty-six. She had been worried that she might not find homes for all of them, but so many townspeople came forward and offered to take them in, there were not enough children to fill the requests.

She left Japan in December 1940, on a ship bound for Vancouver. In the back of her mind was the notion that she would go on to New Jersey, marry the patient Al, and spend the rest of her life with him. But as soon as she got to Vancouver she was flooded with requests to speak, both in Canada and in the United States. One fulfilled engagement led to another, and before she knew it she was involved in all sorts of activities on the West Coast. She helped establish a college movement called the Inter-Varsity Christian Fellowship, and began traveling around organizing chapters in various institutions.

On December 7, 1941, the Japanese attacked Pearl Harbor. Sensei was in Vancouver at the time. Canada and the United States began rounding up all Japanese-Americans and putting them into internment camps. She wrote Al, "I feel I am needed by the Japanese in those camps." He wrote and said, again, that he understood. He was still waiting. He waited until April 1942. Early in that month, Sensei received a telegram telling her that he had died of pneumonia.

When Sensei was telling me this part of her story, her voice did not break or falter; but I noticed that she seemed all at once abstracted, not at all like her usual calm, placid, cheerful self. She said, simply, "Al's death was another clear sign from the Lord—I knew that I had to get back to Japan because He needed me there."

Getting back was not easy. As soon as the war in the Pacific ended, she went to Washington, hoping to get permission to return. Everywhere she went, people misunderstood her motive. "They told me they would send me back right away, as a translator," she says, "or as an interpreter. I couldn't make them understand that I couldn't go in there as a member of the conquering forces."

She went to the Foreign Office in London.

"Nothing doing," said the man she finally got in to see. "No soap, I'm afraid. No way of sending you. Now, why don't you go back to Dublin and get a long, long rest?"

"Will you take my telephone number in Dublin, in case anything comes up?"

"I'll take it—but really, don't get your hopes up, Miss Webster-Smith. There's really no way of our sending you back out there."

Sensei says, "I went to Dublin, praying. That was on a Friday. And again, God provided."

On Monday, the telephone rang. "Miss Webster-Smith, you'd better come and see me," said the voice of the man in the Foreign Office. "It may be that a miracle's happened."

She was in London within twenty-four hours, and the man told her the story of the "miracle." In Tokyo, General MacArthur had announced publicly that he hoped the Christian missionaries would soon return to Japan. Dr. Saiki, hearing of this, wrote MacArthur directly, telling of Irene Webster-Smith's work. MacArthur personally called for her. In February 1947 she was on a ship for Japan, and she landed in April 1947.

"The MPs didn't really know what to do with me," Sensei recalls. "I had a paper that said I could go anywhere and do pretty much as I wanted."

She first went looking for the girls who had been in her home. To her dismay, the first one she found was in a tuberculosis sanitarium, dying; she died ten days after Sensei found her. She went next to Kyoto, where Dr. Saiki had had his maternity hospital. She helped out there, doing what she could, and on week ends she continued to look for her girls. Practically all of them were married, and many had children. To her great delight, she found that all through the war, all had retained their belief and faith in God, and that they were bringing up their children as Christians.

After a time, she decided that her real work lay with young people. She went to Tokyo and rented a room in the university section in which to hold meetings. The room was in the building that also housed the headquarters of the Communist Party, and it amused her to see that her meetings usually were packed while those of the Communists were attended by only a few.

It was while she was working in this section, hoping to get a house where she could set up a real student center, that one of her old girls came down from the north of Tokyo to see her. "This girl had been widowed and had four children," Sensei says. "She was one of the most remarkably courageous persons I have ever known in my life. In that town in which she lived there was no witness for Christ—but that did not deter her from holding services of her own."

The woman asked if Sensei would come up to the town and speak, and she agreed. After the meeting, another woman came up and told her how these meetings had led her to her conversion.

"They have given me great peace," the woman said. "I had been terribly discouraged and unhappy when your 'daughter' led me to Christ."

Sensei nodded happily.

"Yes," the woman went on, "today I am a happy woman despite a terrible sorrow. My husband is condemned to death as a war criminal. We do not know when he is to die—it may be any time. I am allowed to see him for thirty minutes each month. I have tried to tell him about Christ and what He has done for me, but he does not understand."

The woman hesitated. Then, in a trembling voice, she said, "Miss Webster-Smith . . . I wonder if you would take my thirty minutes and see if you can help him?"

The man was in Sugano Prison, north of Tokyo. Most of the war criminals were kept in there. Sensei doubted that she could get in; she knew how stiff the regulations were.

"I don't want to take your thirty minutes with your husband," she told the woman. "But I will see what I can do."

She went to the Army and asked if she might be able to see the man. "No visitors except close relatives," she was told. She persisted, and presently they looked up the man's record. He had been in the Japanese Army; there were many counts of cruelty and conspiracy against him. "He is one of the worst we have in that prison," an officer said.

"He may be one of the worst," she said, "but he's entitled to an interview with some religious person."

The Army made one concession. The officer said he would see if the man wished to have such an interview. The wife, meanwhile, had written him of Sensei's attempts to see him. He said that he would see her if she was permitted to come in.

"It's highly irregular," the officer kept saying. Nevertheless, he arranged a visit.

Sensei told me, "Oh, it was frightening—but I had decided I would not be frightened. They let me through one gate, then another, then another until I was inside the prison proper. Each gate was manned by MPs, and each time they examined my permit. Finally they let me into this long room. There were booths arranged on either side of a heavy mesh wall. On my side there was a little desk and a chair. A GI stood behind me all through the interview—one woman once had smeared poison on the mesh, and her husband had licked it off and committed suicide in that manner."

This man's principal crime was that he had withheld Red Cross supplies from prisoners in a camp of which he had been superintendent. He had been convicted of cruel and inhuman treatment, and there was no chance of his being reprieved.

Sensei started off the interview by telling him that his children were well and happy, and that his wife had found peace in her belief in Christ.

"Yes, I know," the man says. "First, when she came, she railed at me . . . but the last time she seemed changed. And she said she had been converted. That was why I agreed to see you. She had brought me a pamphlet and asked me to memorize part of it."

The part the wife had requested her husband to memorize was John 3:16—'For God so loved the world that He gave His only begotten Son.'

"I have memorized it," the man said, "but I do not understand it."

"Well, at least you've learned that much," Sensei said. "But there is nothing in John's gospel to tell us about the meaning of the name of Christ. We are told that in Matthew."

"What is Matthew?"

"That is another book of the Bible. Matthew was one of Jesus' workers. . . . He told how Jesus came to save people from their sins."

"What sins?" asked the prisoner.

"All sins," she said.

He shook his head. "You cannot know the magnitude of my sins."

Sensei said, "I don't know and I don't care. The blood of Christ cleanses us from all sins."

"What do I have to do to be cleansed?"

"Only this: hold out your hands to Christ and take Him unto you."

"Will you tell me what to say?"

"I'll pray a prayer, and you can follow me."

Sensei prayed a prayer of confession and surrender to Christ, and the man followed her sentence by sentence.

Today, Sensei recalls, "I thought: This man is going to the gallows. I'd better prepare him for death. So I recited from the fourteenth chapter of John: 'Let not your heart be troubled . . .'"

Afterward she said to the man, "Look . . . you've only known Him a matter of minutes, and He's prepared a place for you."

The man was silent; he was deeply moved.

The soldier standing behind Sensei tapped her on the shoulder. "Your time is up."

Disappointment showed clearly on the prisoner's face. But hope showed, too.

"Will you do something for me?" Sensei said.

"What can I do?"

"Try and find someone among your fellow prisoners and tell what has happened to you."

"That would be difficult. They keep us mainly in solitary confinement. We only get a brief period each day for exercise."

"Try to tell *someone*, then."

"I'll try."

She said good-by to the man.

A few days later, Sensei had a telephone call from prison headquarters.

"Do you know a man named Shibano?"

"No. I've never heard of anyone by that name. Why?"

"He is asking for you. He wants to see you."

The first man had told a second. Sensei went to see the second, helped him memorize a few Scriptures, and led him to Christ. That was only the beginning. A few days later, when she was in Kyoto, she had a call from an army chaplain who said that thirteen of the prisoners had asked to be baptized in the Christian faith. "We are here to help Americans, not Japanese," the chaplain said. "They say you have led them to Christ—and will you baptize them?"

By the time Sensei got to the prison, she learned that the chaplains had changed their minds. They had done the baptizing themselves, immersing the seekers in the prison's Japanese bath.

Some days later, Sensei says, she awoke with what the Quakers call a "concern."

"I don't know why it was," she says today, "but I felt that I wanted to see that first man again."

She went out to the prison. "Why do you want to see him?" she was asked.

"I don't know—I only know that I have to see him."

She could hear their derisive mutters: "Isn't that just like a woman . . . she wants something but she doesn't know why she wants it."

"Only the Commanding General can give you permission," she was told.

Sensei went to see the Commanding General. He was sympathetic. "If you really want to see him, and I can see that you do, we'll make a special exception for you."

The General sent her to the prison in his own staff car. The man was brought in as before. He did not know why he had been taken out of his cell. When he saw Sensei, tears came into his eyes.

"What brought you here?" he asked.

"I don't know. I guess the Lord."

"Last night," said the man, "I asked the Lord to send you or my wife. I have some last messages—and I want to confess my sins."

"When are you to die?"

"I don't know. They do not tell us. I have an idea that it is not far off, and I want to be ready."

Sensei wrote down the man's last requests. She sang a chorus of "Nearer, My God, to Thee," read him some verses from her Testament, and prayed with him.

Behind her, the GI guard bowed his head as she and the prisoner prayed.

She said good-by to the man.

As the guard was taking her out of the room, she said, "Are you a Christian?"

"No."

"But you prayed."

"Yes, I did. And I'm not ashamed of it." He paused. "You know, Miss Webster-Smith, there's a change in every one of those men after you leave."

That was a Friday. On Sunday, Sensei was going off to Friends' Meeting, hurrying because she was late, when a British automobile pulled up beside her and the driver offered her a ride. "I recognized you as the lady who's been talking to the prisoners," the man—an army officer—said. "I wanted to talk to you. I was with two men this morning when they were executed. They came out holding their gospels in their manacled hands, singing "Nearer, My God, to Thee." And behind them, others were singing "God Be With You." I wanted to tell you . . . their faces were radiant. Because I saw them, I had to tell you. I want to meet my Maker the way those two men did."

Sensei prayed, and as she did she resolved that she would go on with her work in the prison.

Sensei began by sending Bibles and tracts into the prison. Then, whenever a man asked to see her, she obtained permission for an interview. Some of the men were among the highest-ranking of all the Japanese war criminals. All told, she saw more than one hundred prisoners accept Christ as their Savior.

"I didn't do it," she says. "The Lord did."

She likes to point out the Bible verse which, she believes, was most instrumental in leading the men. It is Exodus 23:20: "Behold, I send an Angel before thee, to keep thee in the way, and to bring thee into the place which I have prepared."

The verse applies to Irene Webster-Smith.

JANUARY 19 § TOKYO TO SEOUL

Once I interviewed and did a story for a magazine about a young soldier from Brooklyn, New York, who had been captured in the fighting in Korea, marched nearly four hundred miles into the North and—after resisting his captors—had been held prisoner in a box the size of a telephone booth for more than thirty months. This young man had said to me, "I used to sit there and remember the terrain we'd been fighting over, and I used to say, 'O Lord, why are we fighting over *this?*'" Now, when I first see Korea for myself—barren, arid, chilly—I remember the soldier's reaction. "It looks like a diseased place," I say to Bob as our plane is about to land us at Seoul.

"It is, now," Bob says. "They've been doing what they can do to recover from the war, and they've made some progress. This year they'll be exporting some rice. If they can ever get their squabble with Japan over the fishing waters settled, that industry may come back. Right now they seem to be at a stalemate. The whole country is having a terrible time recovering, despite all the aid we've given them. There's disease and pestilence everywhere, and filth. I'm told there are two million lepers in Korea, and I can believe it. At Severance Hospital, in Seoul, World Vision is building a clinic and laboratory strictly for the treatment of leprosy and for research into the disease. They've never had anything like it before . . . it isn't much, but it's a start, and maybe some people can be helped. And maybe we can train some doctors to go out and help others. But oh, the task here is so *big!*"

Seoul airport is a collection of square, utilitarian buildings, obviously built by military personnel, still showing boards and squares of olive drab and khaki. A tremendous crowd is waiting, and as we get off the aircraft and it surges forward I realize with surprise that the people are here to meet Bob. A group of about ten men, mostly Korean but including a sprinkling of Americans, detaches itself from the crowd and comes forward, and then we are shaking hands all around and I am desperately trying to remember names—Pastor Han, Pastor Pak, Mr. Kilbourne, Mr. Nelson—and hook them to faces. These are native pastors and representatives either of World Vision or of missionary organizations it helps to support. As we move with our escort toward the crowd, a cheer goes up. Three tiny girls in native costume come forward and give us bouquets of flowers. There is so much confusion and excitement we scarcely notice the bitter wind that lashes in from the north. Our baggage is snatched away from the men unloading the aircraft and we are whisked through customs. Then we are in a parking lot, where a British military vehicle called a Landrover, squat and boxy and obviously springless, is waiting for us. By now I have managed to grasp and hold one young man's name. He is Marlin Nelson, of the World Vision staff, a brisk, efficient man in his mid-twenties, with neatly combed reddish hair, wearing an overcoat and muffler. He looks as though he should be on his way to conduct a Christian Endeavor meeting in some small-city midwestern church. He does not drive that way, however. As soon as we say good-by to the horde of native pastors and get into the Landrover, he throws it in gear and sets off down the road as though he were evacuating us from some dangerous situation.

There is only one paved road between Seoul and its airport. It is barely wide enough for two lanes, and at many points for distances of hundreds of yards it is terraced up twenty or thirty feet above the fields on either side. Neither Nelson nor any of the other drivers we encounter feel that this is dangerous. They all travel at breakneck speed, blasting their horns at pedestrians and cyclists. Some of the cycles are piled high with neatly tied boxes, huge baskets of vegetables and other wares. Once we pass a man with a pig tied on a rack behind his seat. Other people carry huge loads on their heads—boxes, or bundles, tied in sheets. Some of the men wear tall stovepipe hats with wide brims; nearly all the people, men and women alike, are without shoes and are wearing rags bound to their feet. The houses in the fields that we can see are made of mud or clay, with thatched roofs, huddled together for protection from the razor wind. Some of them are built right on the terraces of the roads. "They're owned by people too poor to buy land of their own," Bob says.

A few miles from the airport, Nelson suddenly slams on the brakes and turns into a narrow lane. Before us lies a huge, slanting expanse of brown earth over which a bulldozer apparently has been working. "This is it," Nelson says.

Bob gazes at the field and nods. "Yes, this will be fine." He turns to me. "We're going to build a hospital here—a two- or three-hundred bed one, we hope. There's a desperate need for a children's convalescent hospital in Seoul. You'll see why in a little while, when I show you Severance."

We proceed along the road to Seoul, and as we get nearer the city the number of pedestrians increases by the hundreds.

Presently we cross a long bridge. Below, on the banks of a river, thousands of people are doing laundry, and other thousands are skating on the frozen patches of water. Kids who do not have skates simply sit down on boards and push themselves along.

Tokyo had looked strange to my Western eyes, but only because of the shacks on the outskirts of the city, the open-front shops, the Japanese characters on the signs, and the advertising balloons floating high above the city. Now, in Seoul, the realization that we are in the Far East hits me forcibly for the first time. Tokyo actually is an imitation Western city. Seoul is not; it is every bit as unfamiliar as pictures in geography books I remember from boyhood. The streets literally swarm with people. Dogs run everywhere; every block or so, we see men with five or six goats trotting along on leashes. The shops are all tumbled together in incredible profusion and confusion, all open-fronted, all with platforms on which figures are huddled around brass braziers. Men run along with crates of chickens on their shoulders. We pass a bus, made of old oil drums cut apart and hammered flat; the people in it are packed together more tightly than the poultry in the crates. There are children, children, children everywhere, running loose or standing in clusters in front of the primitive buildings: little girls in bright reds and greens, boys wearing the black jackets and narrow pants and visored caps which, Bob explains, are the uniforms of students.

Presently we come to Severance Hospital. It is a brick building, little more than a shell. The front door is always open, and inside there is a terrible stench that comes from the latrines and from the rotting diseases of the people who come here for treatment. The floors are of cement. Efforts are made to keep them clean, but modern sanitation methods apparently can make little headway against thousands of years of habit. We climb to the fourth floor, where Erv Raetz, World Vision's director in the Seoul office, lies in a room with drab green walls. Raetz, a gentle-faced man in his mid-fifties, slipped on the ice and broke a hip a few weeks before.

"It makes me impatient to be lying here," he says to Bob ruefully. "There's so much to do."

"I want you to lie here as long as the doctor says you must," Bob says, with mock severity.

They pray together. We go out through the gloomy halls.

"Now you see why we need another hospital," Bob says.

Huddled on a bench are a mother and three children. Suddenly, from a nearby room, comes a series of terrible screams. Bob stops a nurse and asks her what is wrong.

"A woman lost her husband. He was run over by a truck. Those"—she indicates the woman and the children—"are relatives of hers. The woman is here to take the widow home, but she does not want to leave her husband's body."

The screams still echoing behind us, we go out and pay a quick visit to the building that has been erected for the leprosy clinic. It is all but completed, and the doctor who will be in charge, a stocky, smiling Korean with a brusque American Medical Association manner, shows it to us with pride. "Here will be diagnosis room," he says. "Here room for treatment." He leads us upstairs. "And here room for research."

"It may not look like much," Bob says, "but it will save some lives." He stops for a moment and closes his eyes, offering a prayer.

We get back into the Landrover, which by this time I have come to loathe as I used to loathe the springless jeeps and weapons carriers I drove in the Army. This machine gives an even rougher ride than they did—and Marlin Nelson still drives as though he thinks we may be executed if we are late. Again I marvel at the lack of concern the pedestrians show for moving vehicles. Once we narrowly miss hitting a brown mongrel.

"You'll notice there are a lot of dogs," Bob says. "That's a commentary on the improvement of conditions in Korea. During the war there wasn't a dog to be found. A missionary who had one was almost certain to have it stolen the second it was out of his sight. People ate them. There was nothing else to eat. Among certain Oriental peoples, dog meat is a great delicacy. They sell it in Hong Kong in the spring, even though the British have been trying to stop them for years. But it's no delicacy in Korea. Here they ate it in desperation."

We arrive at the World Vision compound and are greeted by Nelson's pretty young wife, Kay. The compound was formerly an oil company's staff house; it is made of red brick and is one of the few substantial buildings in the neighborhood. Kay shows me to my room upstairs. She warns me not to drink the water from the taps in the bathroom or kitchen. "All water here must be boiled," she says.

"Don't you find living out here difficult?" I ask.

"It was, a little, at first," she admits. "But I'm used to it . . . and it's what the Lord wants us to do, Marlin and I are sure of that." Self-consciously, as though she feels she has said too much, she slips out the door.

At dinner, Bob listens to Nelson and Mrs. Erv Raetz tell of some of the problems connected with the administration of the 152 orphanages of various denominations that World Vision raises funds to support. Afterward, a long stream of local pastors come in to see Bob—to ask for help, to tell him of the work their congregations are doing, to pray with him. He listens to them patiently and soberly, occasionally making notes on slips of paper and sticking them into his pocket. Every once in a while, when he hears an especially touching story of need, he shakes his head and looks up at the sky, as though imploring God to help. By nine o'clock I am exhausted and go to bed. Bob remains with the pastors until long after midnight. . . .

Next morning, after breakfast, Marlin Nelson takes me out on a short tour of the compound. Marlin tells me a little of his background as we walk along: born in Burlington, Iowa, he was raised on a farm, attended Bethel College, and then went on to the University of Minnesota, after which he entered Fuller Seminary in Pasadena, from which he was graduated in 1955. He is an ordained Baptist minister. While he was at Fuller he met Bob Pierce and became inflamed with the desire to help the World Vision movement. Bob asked him to go to Korea at once, so that the man who was then there, Douglas Cozart, could have a furlough home. Marlin says:

"As a boy, even though I had a missionary sister, I never had any thought of being a missionary myself, let alone a minister. I thought I would be a farmer, like my older brother, and serve the Lord on Sunday; I had the idea about missionaries that so many people have—that they were odd people with eccentric personalities. Well, in college one night at Bethel, the pastor presented the challenge. He said that if we really wanted to work for Christ we ought to at least consider the mission field. I think if that minister had asked me to go and be a garbage collector, I would have done that. I felt the call so strongly.

"I was nineteen. From then on there was a period of waiting and preparation. Meanwhile, I met Kay. She was in training to become a nurse. We figured that it was by the grace of

God that we were getting our education, and that we had no choice but to serve God. We figured we were young, in good health, and if we had those things that others didn't have, and it was possible for us to go and serve, then there was nothing to do but to go. There was a need, and we were ready, and we came."

I ask, "How did your folks feel about your being in Korea?"

His answer comes promptly. "Our folks miss us, naturally, but it's a real joy to them to know we're happy here and happy in the service of Christ."

Marlin takes me first to the World Vision headquarters building at the other end of the compound, to have a look at the Bible Correspondence School.

"My predecessor, Doug Cozart, started this work," Marlin says. "He had come out here for a group called The Navigators. When Bob came through on a trip, met Doug, and saw what he was doing, he thought the work should be expanded. He put it up to the World Vision board, and they voted to underwrite Doug's office expenses. Eventually World Vision assumed the whole expense of printing and distributing those Bible lessons. A couple of years ago, Bob expressed interest in a spiritual program for the orphans World Vision supports, and he asked me to get busy on that. That's my major assignment right now. We called it the Little Shepherd Movement. The program has two parts—evangelization and spiritual growth. The latter includes Bible study and Scripture memory. We provide all the materials for both and push it in all the orphanages. We try to put the whole program on a competitive basis, and offer Testaments as prizes to kids who learn their verses and try to get other kids interested. In our orphanages we have ninety-five hundred kids who are nine years old and older. We feel we can reach those kids—there are ninety-five hundred potential Christian leaders right there. They need spiritual guidance. Many are sponsored in the United States by Christian families; this alone helps to stimulate their interest in Christ. But there are still around twenty-five hundred in the orphanages who aren't sponsored. We've got to reach those kids. We're working with all the Korean churches, encouraging them to help the kids, but again, it's a hard job without sufficient personnel. . . ."

Marlin shows me the shelves on which the lessons are stacked. Several Korean volunteer workers are pulling out lesson-sheets and folding them into envelopes.

"In three months," Nelson says, "we've mailed out around seventeen thousand lessons. We now have about twelve thousand active students, and about that many have finished the course since it was started in 1953. The course consists of nine lessons. A good many people start the course and never finish it, mainly because they don't have the money to pay for postage to mail the lessons back. We hope eventually to send out the lessons with guaranteed return postage. But meanwhile, we think this work is going well. You know, there's tremendous interest in Christ in Korea, perhaps more than in any other Far Eastern land."

Bob Pierce had come in quietly and was listening to our conversation.

"I'll tell you something else," he says. "The Christians in Korea are as devout as those anywhere in the world—more devout, perhaps. When Billy Graham and I were out here in December 1952, I told him about the daybreak prayer meetings. People in Korea get up at 4:30 A.M. to go to their churches and pray—they've been doing it since the days of the Japanese occupation, when they had to do it in secrecy.

Billy couldn't believe it when I told him. There was a church near here just being built. I said, 'Come out with me in the morning and see.' And we got up at that awful hour and went over to the church, and there they were—there wasn't a roof over their heads, they had no walls, there was no floor. Just a scaffolding of a church they were building. They'd each brought along a piece of firewood to sit on. We counted one hundred eighty-nine people there in that church framework. That's why I always say: Korea is the only country in the world where the Catholics wake up to the sound of the Protestant church bells."

We wander over to another building, a larger one which is the headquarters of the Korean Orphanage Program, where Mrs. Florence Raetz is in charge of the orphanage administration.

"Just the job of policing the orphanages is a terrific job," Bob says. "We ask the foster parents in the States for ten dollars a month per child, and it just about costs that to take care of them. That means we have to raise money for the maintenance of the buildings and to pay the staffs. And there's a good deal of other detail work you wouldn't realize at first. Look in this room, for instance."

He gestures toward a room where twelve Korean girls are busy writing at small desks. As we enter, all twelve stand up and smile and bow.

"They're translating letters," Bob explains. "The sponsors in the States like to hear from their adopted children—and the children feel better if they know they have parents across the seas. So we act as a translation clearing house. The child writes a letter, we translate it and send it along, and then when the parent writes back, we send its translation to the child. You know, it's a wonderful thing for the real children of the sponsors to know they have a little Korean brother or sister somewhere out here. Sometimes they exchange snapshots. Sometimes the sponsors will send additional money, so that the orphan can buy candy or something else. When they do send money, we do our best to get the child to send back a bill of sale for whatever is bought, or a picture, or something, so the sponsor will be assured that the child had the use of the money.

"With a hundred fifty-two orphanages and thirteen thousand kids, you can see what a job we've got on our hands."

"We never seem to get done, or caught up," Mrs. Raetz says.

"What makes me feel best," Bob says, "is that before World War II, Korea hardly had a single orphanage. Kids ran loose all over the streets. World Vision can't take all the credit for starting the program out here. Other organizations—such as the Presbyterian groups, the Assemblies of God, The Evangelical Alliance Mission, the Southern Baptists, the Christian Children's Fund, Foster Parents, and the Oriental Missionary Society, to mention only a few—doing a good bit of the job. But we're blessed that we've been able to do what we're doing now." He looks at his watch. "Time to go see General Paik."

§ **THE GENERAL WITH 241 CHILDREN**

General Sun Yup Paik, the four-star Chief of Staff of the Korean Army, turned out to be a stocky, ruddy-cheeked man with a perpetual smile, faultlessly attired in a uniform patterned after that of generals in the United States Army. He welcomed us in his office, served us tea, and at Bob's urging discussed the forces under his command. During his time, he had developed the R.O.K. organization from a ragged band of patriotic enlistees into a first-rate fighting machine, 600,-000 strong, the fourth largest army in the world. General Paik smiled when he told us these facts, but it was obvious that he wanted more to talk about something else, and presently he did.

"How old do you think I am?" he asked me.

I guessed that he was in his mid-thirties, even though I knew that was young for a four-star general.

"I am thirty-nine," he said. "Now," he added, "how many children would you think I have?"

Koreans are prolific, that much I knew. "Three or four?"

"I am the father," said General Paik, with great pride, "of two hundred forty-one children."

Bob laughed loudly at the look of complete incredulity on my face.

"It's true," he said. "Tell him about it, General Paik."

The General began to talk. How he acquired his huge family is a story that goes back to the autumn of 1951, when guerrilla fighters were decimating both United States and R.O.K. troops in the southwestern sector of the Korean peninsula. Many of these guerrillas had drifted down from the north long before the war began, had enlisted the sympathy of unsuspecting natives, and had established strong, well-equipped emplacements in the rocky Korean hills. American patrols were especially vulnerable, since they could not distinguish between friendly and hostile Koreans. As a result, the guerrillas were killing our men by the hundreds.

General James D. Van Fleet called in General Paik, who

was then commanding the First R.O.K. Corps. He did not waste words. "Pull out as many troops as you need," he said, "and get those guerrillas."

General Paik was an ideal choice for the assignment. Born in Pyongyang in 1920 during the Japanese occupation of Korea, he had decided to become a soldier early in life, and had attended the Military Academy in Manchuria in order to avoid serving in the Japanese Army. After the Japanese surrendered to the Allies in 1946 and the Republic of Korea was proclaimed, he had returned to his homeland and joined the Korean Constabulary, which later became the R.O.K. Army. His rise was rapid, and when the Korean War broke out his command, the First Infantry had been responsible for holding the line in the north against the invaders. Van Fleet, aware of his distinguished service and his knowledge of the Korean countryside, gave him a free hand in cleaning out the guerrillas.

Thus began the campaign later called Operation Rat Killer. In three months, General Paik and his forces, comprising two R.O.K. divisions, killed 12,000 guerrillas and took 8000 prisoners.

The trouble was, nobody had anticipated the fact that many of the killed or captured guerrillas were the fathers of small children.

At General Paik's orders—"Remember, we are at war with the Communists, not with their children," he said—the troops began rounding up the parentless, homeless children, sending them to rear areas for care. Efforts were made to find homes for them with Korean families, but in those days of war most of the population was in a state of continual motion, fleeing the battle zones, living in the fields and in those few forests that had not been leveled by artillery.

Before the General quite knew what was happening, he had scores of children on his hands. For a time his men put them up in tents, but that was unsatisfactory for a number of reasons. The soldiers were not nurses; few Korean men know how to care for children at all.

Gradually, General Paik realized that he would have to do something to care for his wards on a more permanent basis. Their number was increasing daily. After consulting with his UN aide, Colonel William A. Dodds, he decided to open an orphanage. He did not know exactly how he would manage it, since he had no money; the pay of even a general in the Korean Army is pitifully small (even as Chief of Staff, General Paik was paid less than $150 per month).

Then a report came in of an abandoned building on the outskirts of the small city of Kwangju. It had been a Japanese brothel; it was subdivided into many rooms. It had been empty for a long time, and it conceivably could be commandeered.

"Take it over at once," General Paik ordered.

The children—by then there were nearly two hundred—were installed immediately. Armed Forces Assistance for Korea contributed funds for remodeling, and General Paik's troops did the cleaning up and carpentry. General Paik called for contributions from his men, and Colonel Dodds raised money from the American troops. In December 1951 the Sun Paik Orphanage was officially opened. The eighty-second Airborne Division then contributed additional funds to keep it open, and General Paik and his men went on sending money from their tiny salaries.

Finally the war was over. General Paik was busy with administrative duties, but not too busy to forget his wards. He asked Armed Forces Assistance again for money, this time to build a school for the orphans—and when the grant was made, he again put his men to work. The completed school, opened at Christmas, 1955, is still in operation today and is attended by the entire orphanage population of 241, and has a Presbyterian pastor as superintendent.

As some of the orphans have grown older and gone out into the world to high school or to work at trades, General Paik has replaced them with other small unfortunates. Troops are still contributing sums of money for the orphans' support, but the bulk of the money currently is supplied by World Vision.

As far as the children are concerned, however, their father is General Sun Yup Paik, as I found out when he took Bob and me to Kwangju. One stormy day we flew there to see the orphanage. All the children were lined up to meet us, the girls in scarlet pantaloons and yellow jackets secured with purple sashes, the boys in slacks and gray-black high-buttoned jackets that comprise the schoolboy's uniform throughout Korea. As we got out of the car that took us from the airport to the orphanage, the children broke into the hymn "This Is My Father's World." Several little girls, their arms full of bouquets, toddled forward to give the flowers to Bob and the General, and the two men bent down and gathered them up in their arms.

"*Abbagee! Abbagee!* [Father! Father!]" the children cried, over and over.

Bob addressed the children through an interpreter, the General said a few words of greeting, and we toured the building, the children clustering after us. The General pointed out the kitchen, the washrooms and the classrooms with his swagger stick; the great smile never left his face. Everything was spotlessly clean.

"They didn't clean it up because they knew he was coming," Bob whispered to me. "When we first were thinking of helping this project, I made a couple of surprise visits here —and it was always like this. It's one of the best-run orphanages in Korea."

When the General left, some of the children cried.

On the way back to Seoul, he told me of his future plans. "My children are growing up," he said. "Near Seoul is a tract of land I have purchased. On it we will put up a trade school for the boys—the girls, of course, will be getting married. But I want them to learn trades, and it is up to me to see that they do have the opportunity." His face was grave yet hopeful. "I do not yet know how I will do it," he said. "But I trust that my God will show me the way, and I know it will be done someday."

JANUARY 20 § TAEGU

"We thought Seoul was bad," my friend Reinhold writes in a letter to his wife after this day is over, "but Taegu! What terrible poverty! Here, people live in holes in the ground, in mounds of mud, under culverts, in gutters. Live? They do not live. They exist."

These are the impressions that stand out as the car takes us from the gravel strip that serves as the airport of Taegu, 150 miles southeast of Seoul, into the center of the city. Presently we stop in front of a two-story brick building big enough to cover the average city block in the United States, a building so substantial and impressive that it is like a mirage in the setting of mud huts and shacks that surround it.

"The Presbyterian church built this hospital in 1899," Bob says. "Presbyterians have done wonderful things here in Taegu. They've got a college, they've got a high school for boys and one for girls, and they've got this hospital. It's got a hundred ten beds in the main building, and there are between forty and fifty in the children's hospital we built a couple of years ago. We now contribute about thirteen hundred dollars a month for care of kids. We also pay the salary of a full-time missionary nurse, Kathy Cowan. It's one of the projects I mainly wanted you to see."

Dr. Howard Moffett, a tall, cranelike man with a face that, considering his angular build, ought to be stern but which actually is as gentle and sensitive as his low voice, welcomes us and takes us up to his office, where most of his doctors are gathered. Most of them are Koreans; the names are all lost to my ears in the wholesale handshaking. "All our department heads have had some training in the United States," Dr. Moffett says. "And all are Christians. They don't have to be Presbyterians, but they must be Christians. This medical work is a wonderful way to get people's ears and bring the message of Christ to them. We're very pleased with the fact that over the years, a total of one hundred twenty-two Christian churches have been founded by people grateful to Presbyterian Hospital.

"You may be interested in hearing what happened here during the war," Dr. Moffett continues. "My last regular report was written in 1950, on the fifteenth of June. That was ten days before the Communist invasion. I went into the service then, and . . . well, never mind about me. The hospital was never bombed, but at one point we did evacuate the whole works to an old Buddhist temple at Pusan. As soon as things quieted down, we came back here. It's funny . . . seven years elapsed before I found time to write another report. Here it is."

He hands me the 1957-1958 report. It begins, "This report includes such things as 6318 blood counts, 233 gastric analyses, and 406 spinal fluid examinations. It has to do with such highlights as 955 decisions for Christ as a result of direct evangelistic work with the patients, and such lowlights as a $15,-000 deficit for coal. In it could be told the story of a fourteen-year-old son of a widowed refugee deaconess, whose eye was so injured by a stone thrown at him in the dark as he went home after church that it could not be saved, but who now has a new artificial plastic eye made and fitted right here in our hospital . . ."

As I put the report in my pocket to study later, Dr. Moffett pointed to a man walking along a corridor. "There's a story in that man. His name is Jin Tae Kim, and he's the ruling elder of a church with a new building program. The congregation had raised all the money it could find, and Jin himself had given two hundred dollars, his life savings. Because he felt he had to contribute more, he came to the hospital in the hope of selling his eye or some other part of his body so that he might make a further contribution to the building fund. When we refused to take his eye, he broke down and wept, saying that after much consideration and prayer he had reached the final decision to make such a sacrifice and that if we wouldn't buy it then he wanted at least to donate it to some needy individual. We still had to refuse, but such an attitude of mind and heart is typical of the willingness of sacrifice, like Abraham's of old, which accounts for the great strength of the church in Korea . . ."

The religious department of the hospital is very active, Dr. Moffett continues. The average of conversions of patients, or decisions for Christ, runs to about seventy persons per month. And not all the conversions are among patients; sometimes whole families move into the hospital with sick persons, and those people also hear the message of the religious leaders.

Now begins a fast trip through the hospital, beginning with the maternity ward. "We don't keep new mothers in here as long as you do in the States," he says. "Three days—that's about as long as we can afford to keep them." He explains that only a very few patients who come for treatment can afford to pay: "We have about six or eight beds for paying patients. The rest is free. It has to be. These people here have nothing. You've seen their houses; you've seen them in the streets."

After leaving maternity, we stop at a door marked OPERATING ROOM. "This is our pride and joy," Dr. Moffett says, flinging a door open. Simultaneously he steps back, startled. An operation is in progress, and a patient under anesthesia is stretched out upon the table while one nurse holds a cone over his face and another stands by in attendance on the surgeon. The latter, his face wrinkling in a welcoming, beaming smile behind his mask, turns away from the skinny-legged body, poised surgical knife in hand, and bows. "*Her-ro, her-ro!*" he says politely, bowing again.

"Better tell him to get back to his work," Bob says hastily to Dr. Moffett. "We can shake hands with him later."

The surgeon looks disappointed as Dr. Moffett closes the door.

"Now to the children's hospital," Bob says. "And I want you to take as much time in here as you need. You won't like some of the things you see . . . but I want you to see them well, so you can tell about them when we get back. There isn't one single thing World Vision is doing that's more important than this project here."

Dr. Moffett is explaining where the child patients come from: "Some are found wandering along roads, some are brought in by the police. If a child becomes very sick, the poverty-ridden family may hopelessly give up all responsibility for it. All over Korea, children are found dead in the streets every day. Many of them die of malnutrition."

Nothing Bob had said could have prepared us for the sights we see in the children's wing. In bed after bed are children, ranging from a month or two up to three years, their bodies covered by multiple abscesses, ugly running sores eating relentlessly at the pitifully weak yellow-brown flesh. "Malnutrition," Dr. Moffett explains. In a crib, standing up and holding to the rail, is a little girl with her right eye bulging like a huge marble, terribly distended and appearing ready to fall out if she shakes her head. "She had a cancer behind her left eye, and we removed that," Dr. Moffett says, "but it's behind the other one now. She can't last long." The baby is smiling. She turns the head with the hideous eye toward us and reaches out her fat little hands. Bob puts his hand on her head and prays aloud. At another crib, Dr. Moffett points to a little black-eyed boy who seems in excellent spirits. "He was a beggar boy on the streets," he says. "He swallowed lye. It burned his throat shut. We've managed to fix it so he can take nourishment, but he'll never talk. We're trying to place him in an orphanage." In another room, two tiny babies, neither more than four or five months old, both suffering from malnutrition, lie in bed with oxygen tubes taped to their noses. "Acute pneumonia, brought on by exposure and malnutrition," Dr. Moffett says. Again Bob prays.

"About twenty abandoned kids are brought in each month," Dr. Moffett says. "A good many are brought in with the umbilical cords still hanging from their stomachs. Some are GI babies, we're sure, but most of them are illegitimate children of Korean parentage. But for those who are brought in there are thousands who die unnoticed."

The impression stands out: all the children, even those most severely afflicted, seem as happy and responsive as their illness and weakness will permit them to be. I mention this to the doctor. "Yes, I believe that's true. As I said, we feel that love is fully as important as medicine. We can't give them as much individual attention as we'd like to, of course—we haven't got the staff for that—but we try to make them feel wanted, and we try to tell the story of Jesus to those who can understand."

Our little party is silent as we go out to the automobile. I look at Reinhold's face and know he is thinking of his own two little girls at home in Pennsylvania.

Dr. Moffett takes us to a baby home, a small frame building on the outskirts of the city. In one room, huddled together on the floor like chicks under a brooder, are twenty babies ranging in age from about six months up to three years. They all smile as we come in; some of them stretch up their arms to be picked up. "These are mostly babies abandoned at City Hall," Dr. Moffett says. "We get them, sometimes, when they're only a few hours old."

"For most of them, this is the only home they ever will know," Bob adds. "There isn't much adoption in Korea at present. The families are too poor. But as the economy gets back on its feet, I'm sure that there will be some. There already are signs that things are improving."

The thought, combined with the sight, is heart-rending.

Over in one corner, a boy of about two is crying. In other rooms there are more children, all sitting close together for warmth—and, the thought occurs, for love. They look at us timidly. They are silent; perhaps they have not learned how to laugh.

One woman takes care of about 115 babies in this home. Neighbors help her, sometimes; visiting nurses from Dr. Moffett's hospital pay her occasional visits. There is nobody else to come to her aid. She does all the cooking, washing and household chores.

"She gets some help from an organization called Armed Forces Assistance for Korea," Dr. Moffett says, "but not much. It's a charity organization the Army set up. They help mainly in building maintenance and construction."

"Where do these kids sleep?" I ask.

"They sleep on the floor," Dr. Moffett says.

"Compared to wartime, these conditions are pretty good," Bob says. "In 1951, when I was here, I found one woman with a hundred babies in a house of three rooms. She had no food, no diapers, no fuel—nothing. I got a sergeant I knew to mislay some cases of milk, and another to find her some blankets. We tried to do what we could for her; I knew the Lord would forgive our foraging to help those babies. It was things like that that brought World Vision into existence. Something had to be done for those babies."

"You see," Dr. Moffett says, "a good many of the state-maintained orphanages, and even some of those operated by churches, refuse to take in babies because they die so easily. They don't want those high mortality rates on their records. The only thing to do is to set up homes like this as a kind of emergency measure. The churches are behind the baby program—there are now one hundred sixty Protestant churches in Taegu."

"It's a measure of the growth of Christianity in Korea," Bob says. "Before the war there were seventeen or thereabouts."

We leave the house and go out into the street to the automobile. It now seems colder than before. Indeed, it struck us this morning that Taegu was colder than Seoul, but our car shoots past any number of people too poor to buy even the rags that serve most Koreans as shoes. Their feet are naked on the frozen ground. "O Lord," Bob says as we pass three barefoot children clad in nothing but thin cotton shirts and tattered trousers, "help us to help these poor people." The three kids smile and wave at us.

Our next stop is the Lighthouse School for the Blind, where four boys and four girls, lined up on benches at the door, greet us by singing "Jesus Loves Me." Their faces are blank, their eyes sunken and sightless, but their voices are sweet and on key, which makes the sight and sound of them all the more touching. Dr. Moffett explains that some of the children here are blind, some are deaf and some are dumb, and some are all three. Yet all are being helped. Some are being helped to hear with mechanical aids. The blind children are learning Braille. Several of them are learning massaging as a trade; throughout Asia, blind persons often earn a living by wandering the streets, offering to give massages with hands and feet. In one room, about twenty boys are sitting together, listening to a man tell a story. The room is all but dark, and I am about to ask why it is kept so gloomy when I realize that it does not matter, to them, how dark it is.

We break out into the sunshine and go on to our next stop,

an orphanage called So Mang, "House of Hope." This orphanage is one of those solely supported by World Vision. It is operated by a man and his wife, and there are fifty-seven children in it. They sleep five to a room, on boards like duckboards raised up a few inches from the floor; the rooms are spotless and well kept. The children, who range in age between three or four and eleven or twelve, are the liveliest and happiest we have seen.

"I'm proud of this orphanage because the kids are so happy in it," Bob says. "The couple in charge have done a wonderful job here."

The children are playing on swings, running after each other in games of tag, bouncing balls and throwing them back and forth. It is like recess in an elementary school in the United States.

Bob calls them together for a word of prayer, and we are off again. Frankly, I am weary. I glance at Bob. He is as fresh as he was when we left Seoul this morning.

"A few miles from here," Dr. Moffett is saying, "there's something you ought to see, Bob. About two hundred people, mostly beggars, are living together in an old, abandoned icehouse."

"Let's go," Bob says promptly.

Despite the horrible sights we have seen this day, nothing in our previous experience has prepared us for the icehouse. It is a huge cement-block shell about thirty yards square; once it had a roof made of hammered-flat oil drums, but that was stolen long ago, piece by piece. The icehouse was constructed by the American Army and abandoned long before the Korean War. Almost at once the beggars of Taegu moved in and began making it fit (so to speak) for habitation. They have plastered mud huts along the inside and outside walls, using everything imaginable as building material—mud and clay, jagged boards, pieces of oil drums and Coca-Cola signs, here and there hunks of sharp glass, rags and bits of canvas. None of the huts has a door; all have flimsy rags over the open entrances. Inside some huts, as many as twenty people are lying on the bare earth floor. Some of them are naked except for diaperlike loincloths; three and four of them lie entwined under a flimsy blanket, tattered and full of holes, their bony arms and legs and sunken chests covered with skin but no flesh, their cheeks sunken and shrunk back so that their skulls are sharply defined. These bodies are all covered with a hard shell of black-brown filth, and for some that is their only insulation against the penetrating, 18-degree cold. The stench in these huts is indescribable, compounded of urine, stool, the filth on the rotting bodies, and the pus that streams out of the infected sores. Word spreads that strangers have come, and slowly the creatures begin to drag themselves out of the huts. Many are too weak to walk, but even the cripples —a legless girl who pulls herself over the hard ground with her hands, a boy with no arms who moves along like a snake —come struggling toward us, all smiling in welcome, all trying wretchedly to be ingratiating. A child leads a barefoot blind woman out to the cluster that is collecting around us. In the middle of this group stands an old, toothless man whose erect bearing indicates that he is the leader, the patriarch. He exchanges a few words in Korean with Dr. Moffett.

"He says there are about two hundred here now," Dr. Moffett tells Bob. "He is not sure how many children—between thirty and forty, he thinks."

Over to one side stands a group of small boys, all barefoot, each wearing only shirts and short summer pants. Seeing me looking at them, one smiles brightly and says, "Hi!" He is proud of his mastery of this American word, and covers his grinning mouth with his hand. "Hi! Hi!" the others cry. Then, overcome with their own mischievousness, they vanish around a corner of the icehouse wall.

Another old man has come up to stand beside the leader. His only garment is a ragged GI overcoat, caught in front with a nail. He has nothing on beneath.

"He says an elder, a Mennonite, has been coming here every morning and holding services," Dr. Moffett says. "And bringing some food."

"What do they eat?" I ask.

"Pieces of flour dough in water," Dr. Moffett says. "Some bean curd every once in a while. If they are very lucky, some rice—but rice costs more than they can afford."

Some of the older people are too weak to come out of the huts. They lie heaped up in doorways, staring at us, trying to smile. Later we learned one actually was dead.

The leader speaks again to Dr. Moffett, who translates: "He says that they could make a living if they had a noodle machine, or a ropemaking machine. But they have nothing, and most of them are too weak to go out and even beg for the money to get a machine."

"Is nobody looking after them now?" Bob asks.

"We've been doing what we can," Dr. Moffett says. "And so have the Mennonites. Last Christmas we took them twenty-five dollars' worth of food. But you know, Bob, every cent we have goes into the hospital."

"I know," Bob says. "Well, we'll see what we can do."

"We've moved fifty of them out and put them in homes or hospitals," Dr. Moffett says. "But as quickly as you move out a group, more come in. This is one of the few places in Taegu where those who have nothing can find a place to live and at least a couple of meals a week. Once, one missionary group tried to get some of them to go to a barber who had agreed to cut their hair and delouse them free. They wouldn't go—they were afraid others would come in and grab their pallets while they were gone. Another time, some people tried to get them to go to the public baths. They wouldn't do that, either. Don't you understand? These miserable huts are the only things they have in the world. They're their security. All they want to do is outwait the cold winter here. That's all they *can* do."

A girl in a blue wrapper, her legs gone from the knees down, pulls herself out of a hut, moving like a wounded insect across the frozen brown earth.

"Look at that girl," Dr. Moffett mutters. "She's been married since she came out here. She hasn't got anything in the world but that blue thing she's wearing; she's without legs, she can barely speak, but someone here wanted her enough to marry her."

Bob, shaking his head, says, "Howie, we've got to do something."

"I know, I know," Dr. Moffett says. "But lack of funds isn't our only problem, Bob. We take tremendous abuse for taking on some projects simply because we can't discipline them. Suppose we put on a regular program of relief for these people—which is unlikely, since we haven't got the funds. As soon as we try to help them, as soon as they get on their feet, they'll be out of here, begging, being public charges again, and the field inspector of missionary work'll come around and see that we have this project on our budget and wonder why we're not controlling it somehow. We can only give them what we can scrape up out of our salaries. My wife goes around over the city all the time doing what she can wherever she can. Once she found a mother and two children living in a packing box. Their skins were cracked open and bleeding from the cold. The mother was an appleseller. She gave them snowsuits for the kids and a coat for the mother out of a relief-clothes box that had come in. The next day she went around to see them and found that they'd sold the clothing to buy apples to sell. That kind of thing happens all the time."

"I know, I know," Bob says sorrowfully. "Our job is to keep our hearts tender to such things. They can't help what they do."

We go back to the compound where the Moffetts live. Nobody says a word on the way; nobody can forget the pall that settled over the faces of the icehouse people as they realized that we had come this time only to look at and not to help them. Yet all had managed to smile and wave farewell.

At tea at the Moffett house, in addition to the doctor and his attractive wife and our party, there is also Mrs. Samuel Moffett. She and her husband, Dr. Howard's brother, have been living in a city called Andong; some months previously, Sam came down with a case of flu which he could not seem to shake, and he is now staying with his brother during his recuperation. Just before dinner, I go upstairs to meet Sam Moffett, who is sitting up in bed, a red bathrobe drawn around his sickness-starved frame. That garment, plus his balding head, gives him the look of a young monk, but there is no monkish placidity apparent on his face. He is impatient to be out of bed and back to his missionary work.

"They tell me you have quite a story," I say. "Let's hear some of it."

"Oh, there isn't much to tell," Sam says. "My father was the interesting member of our family. I haven't done much

at all. I haven't done *anything*." Softly, ruminatively, he begins to tell me about the Reverend Samuel Austin Moffett,
whom the Koreans called "The Looking-up-the-road Man"
because of his habit of walking along with his head held high,
as though looking into the bright future.

In 1889, when the Reverend Mr. Moffett was twenty-
nine, he left his home in Madison, Indiana, to go out to
Korea. There were some missionaries then, but they were
concentrated only in the seaports along the coast. It was death
to go into the interior, everyone said. Moffett chose the dangerous course. He went north to Pyongyang, then called "the
wickedest city in all Asia." As the first missionary ever to
venture into the interior, Moffett was stoned. "I was glad I
was so thin," he would tell his children later. "It made me a
bad target." He moved into a mud hut with a thatched roof
and began talking to the people when he could get them to
listen. They were intensely superstitious. In order to confuse
evil spirits and make them believe that other spirits already
were in power, mothers would name babies Little Squint Eye
or Wart Nose. Moffett gradually began to persuade some of
his neighbors that evil was not the dominant force in life; that
love was. Among those who listened most attentively to what
he had to say was one of the men who had stoned him when
he first arrived in Pyongyang, a policeman named Yi Keui
Poong. He became a convert; more than that, he became the
first foreign missionary sent out by the Korean Presbyterian
Church, of which Moffett became the first moderator.

By 1895, Moffett had so well established himself in the city
that he began buying land. He acquired 110 acres. On that
property, as time progressed, he built a college, a theological
seminary, a Bible institute, churches, and industrial shops. He
spent forty-five years, all told, in Korea, and by 1935, when

he died, there were 1000 churches and 150,000 believers. By then, too, he had seen his five sons follow him into service. Jim is now pastor of the First Presbyterian Church in Oyster Bay, Long Island; Charles, pastor of the First Presbyterian Church in Pikeville, Kentucky; Thomas is pastor of the First Presbyterian Church in Wheeling, West Virginia; and Howard chose to become a medical missionary. Finally, there was Samuel Hugh. Of all the Moffetts, including the father, Sam has had the most adventurous life.

Sam finished his high school studies in Korea in a school set up by his father, then went back to the United States to Wheaton College, Illinois, to study for the ministry. Once ordained he headed straight back for Korea, stayed there briefly, then decided that his real call was in China. He returned to the States once more, studied at Princeton Seminary for three years, then moved on to Yale to take a Ph.D. in Church History. In 1942 he was married, and he and his wife went immediately to Peking, where they enrolled in the language school at the University. They stayed in Peking until the autumn of 1948, when the college disbanded because of the approach of the Communists. Invited to teach at Yenching University, he went there at once. The Communists took over in December 1948. Sam stayed on until October 1949, when he moved to Nanking Theological Seminary. "There weren't many foreigners around China then, and people thought we were Russians," Sam says.

The Communists had taken Nanking in May 1949, but allowed the University to continue in operation. Sam and his wife were held under campus arrest. They decided that if they could they would move on to Yenying, but they did not expect that they would be permitted to go. For some reason, the Communists granted permission, and they moved again. At Yenying they again were placed under campus arrest.

"Every time we turned around, we were interrogated," Sam says. "Also, they tried to get us to attend the Communist study groups."

In June 1950 the Communist pressure upon Sam and his wife became even more intense. Their servants were beaten and tortured. Tradesmen refused to sell them food. They were afraid to venture outside their compound.

"From June until Christmas, things kept getting tighter and tighter. We had great difficulty getting food. We could not hold classes or services. Our sympathetic neighbors tried to help us, but they too were afraid of the Communists.

"At Christmas I telegraphed Hong Kong asking for money. It came through. I put it in the bank in Yenying, then drew it out."

The Communists had kept accusing Sam of espionage activities. His handling of the money now gave them an excuse to substantiate their claim. In the middle of January 1951 they took him to the police station, arrested him, and charged him with embezzlement and organizing a spy ring. After four days of interrogation, they finally gave up. Anxiously he returned to his compound; for all he knew, his wife also had been taken into custody. To his intense relief, she had not been harmed.

After a few weeks, another Chinese official came to Sam's house and told him that he was to be deported. He and his wife were sent out through Hong Kong. From there they made their way to the United States, where Sam rested a year and then entered Princeton Seminary again, as an instructor. In January 1955, his wife died in Princeton. Alone, all but brokenhearted, he decided that he had to go back to the Far East and live out his life in service to God, as his father had done. His brother Howard was then in Taegu and he decided to join him. He went to Korea in the fall of 1955.

That summer, just before leaving, he had met a young girl in Princeton—Elizabeth Tarrant, from Columbia, South Carolina, who had been attending Wheaton College. Once Sam arrived in Korea, he began corresponding with her. By the middle of 1956, Sam's work with the Koreans in Taegu had refreshed his energies. He felt like a young man again and was ready to branch out from Taegu and find a field of his own to work in. Simultaneously he felt that he needed a wife to work with him. He wrote Elizabeth Tarrant and asked her to come out to Korea to marry him. She accepted.

Sam and his wife are now living in Andong, where he is studying the Korean language and working with the some three hundred churches in the area. He supervises the activities of forty native pastors who work with those tiny churches. I ask him why he had decided to go back to the Far East. "I don't know," Sam says. "I guess I was just born to be a missionary. I felt I didn't fit in the United States. There are so many people who can teach at Princeton . . . but so few who can come out to Korea. My father used to say, 'Don't become a missionary if you can possibly help it.' He felt the life was too hard. I thank God I never took his advice."

Downstairs, they are calling us to come to dinner. Mrs. Howard Moffett has set out a fine meal, including a tinned ham she has been saving just for company, and a plate of the local fermented-cabbage dish called *kimchi*. Bob, Reinhold, and I have enormous appetites, but none of us is able to do justice to the fine food—the terrible sights we have seen that day are still too fresh in our minds.

Presently Bob lays down his fork. "Howie," he says, "we've got to do something about those poor people at the icehouse *right now*. What can we do?"

"The best thing," Dr. Moffett says, "would be to get them some underwear."

"They'll sell it," Bob says.

"I don't think so. I think they would appreciate it more than anything—the cold seems to be bothering them more than lack of food."

Mrs. Moffett says she will go out to the icehouse and make a head count. Dr. Moffett, springing up from the table to get his hat and coat, says he will go to the market and find out the cost of underwear. Bob has his personal checkbook out. "Come on, you men," he says to Reinhold and me. "Chip in. We've got to set up our own personal organization and help those people."

Next morning our automobile, loaded with bundles of underwear Dr. Moffett bought in the Taegu market, sets out for the icehouse at eight o'clock. What I see now seems even more terrible than it did the afternoon before, for at that time my senses already had been numbed by the pitiful sights at the children's hospital, the house for the blind children, and the baby home. Now I seem to be seeing the icehouse for the first time, noticing the piles of human excrement everywhere, the torn paper-and-lath windows in the mud huts, and the utter misery of the people who live in them; in the fresh morning air, the stable stench of this place is all but overpowering. The people struggle out of the huts again as the wild-animal boys hail our arrival. I notice more details: most of them have bits of thread and pieces of mattress stuffing in their hair, and they are clothed in tatters even worse than I remember from the day before. Those who are not barefoot are wearing thin rubberized slippers, or rags, and those who have the slippers have no socks. A girl with a clubfoot hobbles out and joins the gathering crowd. Her foot is covered with festering sores. An old man, so crippled in one leg he can walk only sidewise, leaning on a jagged, splintery stick, is clad only in a torn T-shirt and a pair of thin linen trousers. A woman has two terry cloth towels wrapped around her, one for a blouse and one for a skirt.

Miss Lillian Ross, a missionary Bob met when he first arrived in Korea, has come along with us this morning. Looking at the icehouse people lining up, Bob says to her, "You know, Lillian, that first time you took me to that baby home, you certainly started something in my life." He turns to me. "It was my second trip to Korea, after Seoul had fallen in the war. I was traveling as a correspondent, and I reached Taegu. I stayed with the Reverend Arch Campbell, a Presbyterian. Arch was the only missionary left in the city—everybody else had gone, but he felt he had to stay to share the plight of his Korean flock. He never did leave. He stayed out the whole war. Well, at that time the city was crammed with people, refugees . . . it was winter, kids were dying all over the place. Miss Ross was there, too, and she took me out and showed me one of the houses where they were trying to do something for the babies. . . ."

Bob turns back to the business at hand. Lee Sang Bo, the elder who has made caring for these icehouse people his burden, is standing by.

"Howie," Bob says to Dr. Moffett, "ask him what we can do for them that will help them get on their feet a little bit."

Dr. Moffett confers with the elder in Korean for a few minutes, then turns to Bob. "He says that either a vermicelli-making machine or a ropemaking machine would help them earn some money and get some food."

"Let's get them both," Bob says. His checkbook is already out, and he is unscrewing the cap of his fountain pen. Resting the checkbook against my shoulder, he writes out a check and gives it to Elder Lee.

We distribute the underwear. Dr. Moffett has bought a variety of sizes, beginning with the smallest—but not up to the largest. There are no large-sized people here.

The icehouse people are laughing and chattering excitedly as Miss Ross and Mrs. Moffett pass out the clothing. They hold it up to their skinny bodies. One boy begins to put on his suit over the clothes he already is wearing. On the ground, the legless girl tries to pull the legs over her arms. The noise and excitement are so great that they attract other people who live in huts alongside the road that leads to the icehouse. They stand in a fringe around the icehouse people, their faces drawn and wistful. In Korea, there is no end to the need. "If we'd got forty times as many pairs, we still wouldn't have had enough to pass out to everybody who lives in this neighborhood," Bob says.

Presently all the underwear is distributed. The elder says something to Dr. Moffett in Korean, and the doctor says to Bob, "They want you to say something to them."

Bob nods, and Elder Lee assembles the people in the "court" of the icehouse. Bob stands on the steps and says:

"We bring you greetings. We come from far away, over the sea, from America.

"The people of our country want to be friends with you people. We love you. We want you to know that Jesus Christ loves you.

"As a token of our love and friendship, we bring you these clothes.

"We also will help you to get a machine, so that you can support yourselves.

"We are not giving you these things. Jesus Christ is giving them. When your elder brings you the Word of Jesus Christ, listen to him. Take His Word into your hearts.

"May God bless you and keep you."

The elder leads the icehouse people in a hymn. At the close of it, they all wave and shout "Peace!"

"Peace!" Bob says, waving back. "Bless your hearts."

JANUARY 21 § TAEJON

At Taejon, the airstrip, built by the United States during the Korean War, has been let go; there is little traffic in or out of this small city, and the headquarters building for the airport is little more than a shack. As usual, native pastors have come out to meet us. So has Elmer Kilbourne of the Oriental Missionary Society; he came down from Taegu the night before. This is Elmer's special domain, this area around Taejon, and he is eager to show us what he and his fellow workers have been doing. Elmer is a thickset, brisk man in his early thirties with short-cropped curly dark hair. His manner is in striking contrast to that of Marlin Nelson; Nelson is reticent and contemplative, while Elmer is forthright, almost pugnacious, in his service of the Lord.

"Come on, come on," he says to the native pastors, who are bowing and shaking hands and smiling, "these men have got things to do." He herds them into one automobile and our party into another. He drives as everybody in Korea drives—straight and fast, oblivious of the spring-breaking bumps and ruts in the dirt roads.

"This place we're going to," he throws over his shoulder, "is our Boys Town. It's for delinquents. We modeled it on the famous Father Flanagan's Boys Town in America. It's frankly an experiment, but it seems to be working out."

We arrive at the Boys Town within five minutes. All along the lane leading into it, on either side, the boys are lined up, more than three hundred strong. Each is wearing the now-familiar black schoolboy's uniform, and each has had his head shaved. As we draw closer, they all bow—and then I notice that some seem to be wearing parts of Boy Scout uniforms. But I cannot be sure.

"They're Boy Scouts, all right," Elmer says. "We've got two troops of Scouts here. We offer membership in the Scouts as incentive for work and good behavior."

The frame building needs paint. It looks as though it has been standing a long time. Actually, it is not old. It was put up by the Korean government and by UN funds in 1956, after World Vision bought a thirty-acre tract and turned it over to the Oriental Missionary Society to use. The reason it looks older is its need of a coat of paint, plus the hard usage it has taken from the boys.

"These are tough kids," Bob says. "Nearly all of them are orphans. Nearly all of them were picked up by the police for thievery, for pimping, for picking pockets and other crimes. They were forced into those crimes just to survive. Did you know that more than fifty per cent of the crimes in Korea are committed by kids under eighteen? It's one of the worst problems the government has."

Elmer says, "Even when we get them in here, it's hard to break them of their bad habits at first. Look at the vandalism. They're savages, many of them. They steal light bulbs, they even steal food from each other. They range in age from eight to fourteen, and some of the older ones who come in here are just too far gone for us to help much. But God is able!"

We look over the grounds, crowds of the boys following us everywhere, giggling, pointing at our strange clothes, trying to get a better look at Reinhold's camera. "Over there," Bob says, pointing to some fields behind the main building, "they've got their own garden. They grow nearly all their own food. They've got some fruit trees back there, too."

"And they're raising rabbits in the back," Elmer adds.

The man in charge of the Boys Town is Kim, an elder in the Oriental Missionary Society Church. His helper is Mr. Cho. "There's a heartbreaking story in Cho," Bob says. "He's a refugee from North Korea. He had to get out because he was a Christian, and he came down here during the war. He can't go back. He hasn't seen his wife and children for nine years. He doesn't even know if they're alive. Now these boys are his children."

Elmer, leading us quickly through the buildings, says, "These kids are organized into their own self-governing unit. They have a mayor, a council, an executive committee, and they discipline themselves, have their own bank, appoint committees for cleaning up. Considering the fact that so many of them were incorrigibles, it's amazing. You know, because they're from the criminal element, it's hard for us to find sponsors in the States for them. People hesitate to take them on the way they do other orphans because they're afraid the kids will go over the hill. But we've managed to find sponsors nevertheless—two hundred and forty out of the three hundred boys are being supported by people in the States. And, funny thing, some of them are being supported by a bunch of prisoners in the Nebraska State Prison. A couple of lifers are on the sponsoring committee to support these kids. Poetic justice—criminals trying to give bad kids a break.

"We're pretty sure nearly all the kids respond well to the treatment. In the three years this home has been in existence, we've had five of the older kids go into military service. The reports back on them have been very favorable."

Our tour completed, the energetic Elmer whisks us off to Taejon proper. On the outskirts of town, in a shack, a woman is standing over a steaming kettle, ladling out what appears to be corn meal to individuals who stand waiting in a line. From the look of their clothes, these people are nearly as destitute as those we saw in the icehouse in Taegu. This is one of 130 feeding stations the Oriental Missionary Society— O.M.S. for short—has set up throughout Korea, distributing surplus food shipped in by the United States government— flour, corn meal, milk and cheese.

"We don't know why they send so much cheese," Elmer says. "Koreans don't eat cheese. It just goes to waste unless we can disguise it somehow, combine it with some other food. But they keep sending it. It seems to me they'd do better sending it to some country where the people would appreciate it. The trouble is, it often seems to me, so few of the people in charge of administering the aid programs for foreign countries have any understanding of the needs of the countries. Anyhow, we do what we can with what we have,

and we're grateful for it. In our O.M.S. stations we're feeding twenty-eight thousand people a day. At least we're doing
that much."

It seems to me that the townspeople in Taejon seem to be
even worse off than those in Taegu.

"This whole town was rubble during the war," Bob says.
"Six thousand people were murdered and buried in one
mass grave here."

Near the feeding station is an O.M.S. orphanage with 156
children living in it. "Interesting thing about the orphanage,"
Elmer says. "We've got a Buddhist nun helping out in it.
Some of the kids found her up in the hills. She had no place
to go, and we asked her if she wanted to come and live and
help out with the kids, and she said she did, so she's living here.
The services are Christian, of course, and we're hoping that
someday we'll be able to lead her to Christ."

Elmer leads us to the automobiles again, and we bucket
across the town to the opposite outskirts, where he abruptly
turns onto a terraced road so full of ruts the car threatens to
careen off the sides at several points. After about a mile we
come to a hole. It is so deep that we all have to get out of the
vehicle so that the driver can negotiate it successfully.

"I'd hate to come in here when it's raining," Bob says.

"*Nobody* comes in here by car when it's raining," Elmer
says.

Our destination is the Taejon Leper Colony. It is a cluster
of white frame buildings on a hill, and as we approach it we
can see figures coming out to greet us.

"These lepers in this colony had been living in holes in an
abandoned graveyard," Bob explains, "until Elmer and the
O.M.S. got busy with the native pastors to get them a house
to live in. About ninety-eight per cent of the six hundred

lepers in the colony are now churchgoers. World Vision built them a little chapel. That is, we supplied the funds. They built it themselves. They do everything themselves—nobody else will help them because everybody's so afraid of the disease."

Elmer Kilbourne says to me, "That's the worst part of leprosy, looking at it one way. It's the social ostracism connected with it . . . and it happens not only here; it happens all over the world, wherever there are lepers. Leprosy can be arrested. In many cases it can be cured. But even though a man may survive it, once he has been driven out of his village or out of his home, he can't go back. His relatives, friends, and neighbors simply will not accept him. So he has to live with other lepers. The people simply do not understand that it's rare for an adult to catch leprosy from another. The disease seems to be communicable primarily to infants."

We pull up at the buildings and the lepers come to meet us, keeping at a respectful distance. Their faces make a revolting frieze of pain and decay; almost to a man, their noses are sunk into their skulls, and their ears are unnaturally thick and distended.

One of the native ministers, Pastor Lee, has made this colony his special burden. He leads us on a tour of the grounds and shows us inside the little chapel, which is as clean and neat as any we have seen thus far in Korea. At one point during the tour I brush against one of the lepers. He jumps back, jabbering apologies, bowing and shaking his head, trying with pathetic eagerness to tell me that he did not mean to touch.

"You see," Elmer whispers, "that is the terrible part. They feel they are unclean because they don't really understand the disease themselves. They are as superstitious as the people who shun them. They think they can communicate the disease to others, and it is useless to try to tell them that the chances are good that they could not give it to another adult."

Some of the lepers appear perfectly normal; but under their shirts and trousers are large areas of anesthetized skin or boils that will erupt and eat away flesh and bone. Yet they are cheerful. They are as hospitable as they can be under the circumstances in which they are forced to live. I look at one man, a fellow who must have been handsome until the disease began to consume his nose, and I wonder what he must think about as he lies on his hard board bed at night. All of us manage to postpone all thoughts of our own deaths as long as we are reasonably healthy and functioning. Even many cancer victims these days can know *some hope*. This man knows vaguely that his disease perhaps could have been arrested, by means it is not in his power to fathom, let alone to understand. He cannot be certain how slowly or rapidly it will consume him. And so he lies staring up into the darkness. I begin to understand why so many of these lepers have become Christians. Man must exist on illusion or on faith, and the native pastors and their backers, the O.M.S., have offered them the road to faith. I also understand why they have labored so diligently to make their little colony beautiful. In work there is diversion, and also there is hope. Yet these thoughts are almost too much for me, and I am relieved when it is time to push on to the next stop.

Still, I cannot get the things I have seen during the past day and a half out of my head. I have always been interested in the countries in Asia, and before coming out here I read a good deal about the people and the places we are visiting and will be visiting. Nothing I read managed to communicate to me the poverty, the hopelessness, the frustration of these people; nothing showed me the superstition, the need, the value of things that to a Westerner are valueless. All my life I have supported do-good causes, helping to send money and clothes to the underprivileged of the world, without having the least sense of what those acts might mean to them. It was not until I saw the people in Seoul, the families living in holes in hills and in packing boxes and in barrels, that I began to understand the real gulf between our civilization and theirs. My own world is one in which security, or even the idea of security, is never questioned—and security means enough to eat, a roof, friends. Out here the idea of security does not exist. They never have known it.

Now we are visiting a place dear to Elmer Kilbourne's heart—the Ruth Widow Home. "There is no hope for a widow in Korea," Elmer explains as we approach this neat compound. "If a woman loses her husband and has children, she is doomed to a life of supporting them as best she can. The harassed government will support her for two years— after that, she's on her own. We've been setting up these houses where widows and children can stay together, and in the time that they're with us they can learn to sew or to do some kinds of handicraft that will enable them to support themselves when they're turned loose."

The widows live in tiny cubicles, separated one from another, in barrackslike buildings. Some have three, four, and five children. They are all diligently at work on sewing machines that World Vision has provided for them, making uniforms, house dresses, and other utilitarian garments, most of which will go to the Korean government. They also are taking clothes sent by relief organizations and altering them so that the people meant to use them will find them more suitable. These people are as happy as they can be within their own private emotional frameworks. They have found something they can learn and do which also will be useful later when the government no longer will pay for their support.

"We have a Bible Training Course we're using with these women," Elmer says. "And the good part of it is, most of them respond to it. We've got about fifty of these homes that we're helping along, and out of them will come a lot of workers for the church."

On the way back to the airstrip, I ask Bob how he can explain the tremendous Christian activity in Korea. He hesitates. "Well, one reason, of course, is the missionary work of the Kilbournes and the Moffetts and people like them who have been active here for more than fifty years. But also, there was the war. You know, the Korean War was one of the most terrible of all time. It decimated this country and left it hopeless. It was bound to happen that many hundreds of thousands of people would turn to Christ. But there was much Christian feeling before, more than most people realize. And the war could not drive it out of the people, no matter how much they suffered. Oh, the stories I could tell! But let me tell you about just one man. His story isn't typical . . . but it's representative of the spirit of the Koreans who have accepted Christ. His name was Pastor Im. . . ."

§ "I WILL NOT SELL MY SOUL . . ."

Pastor Im had a small church in a village in North Korea when the Communists began taking over the government. For a long time they ignored him; he went on conducting his services as usual, praying that he could keep on bringing the Word to his people. But after a year, realizing the strength of the Korean Christian church, the Communists began trying to use it as an instrument of propaganda. Ministers who refused to preach Communist doctrines to their flocks were taken out of their homes at night and beaten. Some of them never were seen again.

One day Pastor Im's turn came. A Communist official went to his house and gave him his orders.

"I cannot tell my congregation those things," he said, "because they are contrary to the Word of God."

"The same thing that happened to the others will happen to you."

"Let it happen."

"You will be killed."

"You can destroy my body, but you cannot destroy my soul."

"We'll do away with your family."

Pastor Im thought of his beloved wife and two children. He hesitated. Then he said, "What you do is between you and God. I would rather have my wife and babies die at the gun and know that they and I had stood true to God, than to sell my soul to save them."

The Communists took him away one night and threw him into prison, into a dark room with thirty others. They kept him there for two years, during which time he never had a chance to wash, shave, or change his clothes. His only food was the bowl of slop they gave him each day. Yet his spirit never faltered. He kept up his hope by reciting to himself, over and over, the Bible verses he had committed to memory. "Believe on the Lord Jesus Christ and thou shalt be saved," he reminded himself in the words of Acts 16:31, and he found comfort in "What I do thou knowest not now; but thou shalt know hereafter" (John 13:7).

In September 1950 the UN forces poured across the 38th Parallel into North Korea. Among the prisoners they released was Pastor Im. The first time in more than two years that he had seen sunlight, his only thought was to get to his family. He set out on the road, heading southward.

The UN forces were rounding up everyone who had no identification. Pastor Im had none. He thumbed a GI truck for a ride, and a soldier hauled him aboard. He explained that he wanted to get back to his village, but instead he was taken three hundred miles below the Parallel and thrown into another prison. This one was better than the first. He was given a bath, a shave and a new suit of clothes with the letters PW on the back.

"But I am not a Communist," he protested. "I never was. They put me in jail because I resisted them."

"Yes, yes," said one of his guards. "We've heard a thousand stories like that. You Communists will lie as soon as breathe. You're from North Korea, and that's enough."

Pastor Im tried to find out what had happened to his family, but he was told that there was no way of getting a message up north. His spirits sank lower and lower, but somehow he retained his faith and hope.

On Christmas Eve of that year, he got together with some other Christians with whom he had become acquainted. He suggested that they sing some hymns, and went to a guard and asked permission. The guard said, "All right . . . but don't make any trouble."

Pastor Im and a handful of men gathered in one corner of the barbed-wire enclosure in which they were kept and began singing carols: "Silent Night," "It Came upon a Midnight Clear," "Hark! the Herald Angels Sing," and others.

As they sang the old songs, a great peace came into Pastor Im's heart. He later said that it was as though he knew, in that instant, why God had sent him into the camp.

The Communist prisoners were muttering angrily. Some protested to the guards. Others moved in upon the group and made threatening gestures.

Pastor Im and his friends went on singing. The sound of their voices attracted other men, and soon a huge crowd had gathered—some to listen, some to join in, and some to stand and stare in amazement at the courage of this group of Christians in professing their faith in a camp made up largely of antagonistic elements.

Two and a half hours later, the guards finally broke up a crowd of 4000 men who were listening spellbound to Pastor Im telling of his belief.

The story of Pastor Im spread from the camp and reached some American missionaries who had been made chaplains and asked to stay on in Korea during the fighting. The missionaries, in turn, requested permission to go into the camps.

"Impossible," an official said. "You would be killed. The men in that camp are mainly Communists, and they hate Christians."

The missionaries insisted. "The Geneva Convention insures any man of any nation the right to worship as he pleases—and in addition to Pastor Im, there are at least half a dozen other Christians in that camp."

The officials relented. Two UN chaplains were assigned to the camp. They immediately got in touch with Pastor Im and received permission for him to have the freedom of the area. Before long he was conducting church services. A bit later, when men began dying by the hundreds from disease and malnutrition, he undertook to conduct funerals. Then he began trying to do something about curtailing the spread of disease. With the chaplains' help he set up a number of hospital tents.

The movement spread to other camps. By the summer of 1951, 167,000 prisoners were listening to the gospel in the Korean prison camps. In many of them, as many as 12,000 were rising each morning at six o'clock to attend prayer meetings. Pastor Im never saw his wife and family again, but he was serene in the knowledge that by remaining true to his belief he had become an instrument of the Lord.

JANUARY 23   §   SEOUL

We are back in our room at the World Vision compound. Reinhold is fussing with his cameras and I am writing a letter when Bob comes in. He sits down on the edge of a bed. "I hope we're not going too fast for you fellows."

Reinhold and I are bone-tired. He says, "Shucks, Bob, we were just complaining to each other that you don't move fast enough."

"You guys," Bob says, grinning. Then he becomes serious. "Maybe you're beginning to understand why I wanted you to see some of these things out here. Maybe you can understand now why Korea is so close to the hearts of all the World Vision people."

"What makes me angry," I say, "is the attitude of our government people—the ones we've met. They're here to help, and yet they seem to feel resentment."

"Be patient with them," Bob says. "Be forgiving. There's so much to be done—and so few people to do it. But those who are trying are doing wonderful things. Tonight you'll talk to the Kilbourne family . . . now, there's a family for you. I met the Kilbournes the first time I went to China. I landed in Peking to speak in a Union Conference for Young People in a Methodist church, and I was put in the Oriental Missionary Society compound to live while I was there. That was where I first met Elmer Kilbourne and his twin brother, Ed. They were studying then, but even while they were students they were working hard to spread the Word. They had a daily broadcast over a station in Peking—a closet-sized station. They broadcast in English, and the Chinese students listened to them to improve their language studies. For three years I went back there to hold meetings in Peking. I never see a picture of Mao addressing mobs by the old palace in the center of the city without remembering the days when the Kilbourne boys and I held services there on the same spot with crowds of ten and fifteen thousand. That was in 1947 and 1948. I was last there in November of forty-eight . . . the city fell in January forty-nine. When the Kilbournes finally left, the Communists were already in the city. The plane landed on the airstrip and kept the motor running, and they got out just ahead of the Reds. It's some family, the Kilbournes. . . ."

The story of the Oriental Missionary Society, I learned, began over sixty years ago in Chicago, and began with Ernest A. Kilbourne and Charles Cowman, division chiefs in the telegraph company. Neither man was religious, and if anyone had suggested that they might someday become missionaries, they would have laughed. Then, one night—no one remembers exactly when it was or how it happened—Cowman's wife happened to go to an evangelistic meeting. She was so struck by what she heard that she went back a number of times. After a while she became a Christian herself and led her husband to the Lord. The serenity Cowman found caused him to attempt to communicate something of his experience to his friend Kilbourne, and the latter became Cowman's first convert.

The two men joined the Methodist church. Mere church membership, however, was not enough. They wished to learn more so that they could teach. Both had been working on the day shift at the telegraph company. In order to attend classes at Moody Bible Institute, they requested transfers to the night shift. At Moody they heard many returned missionaries speak of their work, and it occurred to each of them that it would be a wonderful thing if they could duplicate the work of the Institute in foreign fields. They applied to the Methodist church to go forth as missionaries with that specific project in mind, and were at first accepted. Later, some official in the church decided that it could not back such a project at that time.

Still, the call was so strong in them they decided that they would go out on their own. At that time missionaries of the Protestant church had been in Japan for only about forty years, perhaps even less, and had made almost no impact upon the Japanese. If ever there was a field ready for their efforts, it was Japan. Each man had a little money—just about enough for passage for himself and his family. Cowman went out to Japan first, in 1901. Kilbourne, his wife, and two children followed in 1902. Kilbourne arrived in Japan with five dollars in his pocket. Yet each had managed to interest some friends in their great scheme, and they trusted in God to provide the funds they would need to carry it out. Also, Kilbourne had spent the year before his departure raising money enough to see them through the year.

In Tokyo, the two men set up their headquarters in downtown Tokyo, near the Ginza area. They decided upon the name Oriental Missionary Society, and outlined a three-year training course. They advertised for students, and a handful came. Four years later, they sent out their first missionaries. Because they were not formally affiliated with any organized church, they instructed their workers to encourage the Japanese to set up Christian churches under their own indigenous names. That is why, today, there are O.M.S.–founded churches throughout the Far East (and throughout the rest of the world) bearing names that apparently have no affiliation—the Korean Holiness Church, the Evangelical Church of India, the Japanese Holiness Church, and so forth.

"The idea behind our program," Edwin Lawson Kilbourne, known as "Uncle Bud," told me, "is to help the natives to help themselves."

Uncle Bud, a slight, erect man with a handsome face, now sixty-five, was eleven when his father took his family to Japan. As I write this he has just retired to live in the United States. He is a man of enormous energy, as his father must have been. So are his sons, Ernest, and the twins, Elmer and Edwin W. The indefatigable spirit of the Kilbournes is infectious, and it is easy to understand why Bob Pierce originally was attracted to them and they to him. These people are bustling builders, pioneering and self-reliant. And promoting.

"Elmer Kilbourne could charm the birds out of the trees,"

Bob Pierce once said to me, and the truth of the cliché was borne out one afternoon in Korea while we were visiting some of the O.M.S. installations. We were all tired and cold and in need of refreshment. In Korea there are no wayside snack bars or road stands where one can fall in for a coffee break. We happened to be passing an army post. Abruptly, Elmer Kilbourne steered the vehicle through the gates and pulled up in front of a mess hall. He darted inside and was out in five minutes. "The mess sergeant'll give us a cup of coffee," he said. We went inside, and the mess sergeant (who was right out of Central Casting, even to the extent of paring his fingernails with a pocketknife) bade us gruffly to make ourselves at home while one of his private slaves brought us coffee and cookies.

Uncle Bud Kilbourne, after spending most of his teens in Japan, returned to the United States in 1909 to enroll in John Fletcher College, in Oskaloosa, Iowa, and after marrying his childhood sweetheart in 1915, went back to Japan. His father decided that he had better set out for Korea, to get the work of the O.M.S. established there. In 1907, some Koreans had graduated from the O.M.S. Institute and had returned to their native land, but they needed help in carrying on their work. As soon as he got to Korea, Uncle Bud began overseeing the construction of the buildings for the O.M.S. Institute.

"Almost as soon as we were ready to begin," he recalls, "we got sixteen students from China—eight men and eight women. That was what we wanted. We hoped to train them, send them back to China, and eventually go in there ourselves and found an institute."

Word of the O.M.S. activities in Japan and Korea got back to the United States, and more support began coming in. This encouraged the elder Kilbourne and Cowman to decide to send young Edwin to China to begin the work there. Cowman did not live to see the inauguration of the Chinese project; he died in 1924. The following year, Uncle Bud went to Shanghai, where he bought some land and began doing all over again what he had helped start in Korea. Before the program was terminated, he had established three Bible seminaries in China —in Peking, Shanghai and Canton.

The Japanese moved on Shanghai in 1937. Uncle Bud had evacuated his family and his office staff to Korea but chose to stay on himself. "I couldn't let anything happen to what we'd worked so hard to build," he says. Shanghai then was a city within a city—a Chinese city surrounded by an international colony. Uncle Bud moved into the YMCA, which was in the international part. From his room on the ninth floor he could see the fighting clearly. "Oh, the kids thought it was a circus," he says today. "They never forgave me for not letting them stay on to watch. The Chinese left five hundred troops behind to cover their retreat. They were terrifically outnumbered by the Japanese. They held out for five days, and finally were ordered to surrender by their superiors in Chungking, but they fought their way out of that warehouse and about three hundred of them did make it out.

"I tried to do what I could during the fighting—errands of mercy and so on," Uncle Bud continues. "Once a missionary lady I knew got permission from the Japanese to go inside their lines to her house to get some stuff she needed. She was gone several hours, and finally the people in her mission came to me and asked if I could get her out. So I drove in, in our truck. The house was three doors from the front line of Japanese trenches. A bunch of them came at me with bayonets. I said, 'I beg your pardon, I've come here to get a lady who's in that house.' She came out on the porch and she said, 'Oh, have you come to take my stuff out for me?' There were bullets whistling all around, but she didn't seem to notice them. Well, the Japanese wouldn't let her have so much as a toothbrush. They said to me, 'You'd better take this lady and get out of here,' so I put her up on the seat of the truck and drove out of there."

Uncle Bud got his family back from Korea when the fighting subsided and went on with his work. The Japanese did not molest him until Pearl Harbor Day—when, along with all other Americans in Shanghai, he was thrown into an internment camp with his wife. The boys were home in college at that time. "Actually, it wasn't so bad," he says. "As soon as I got into the camp they made me head interpreter, and I became a kind of liaison officer. It wasn't too bad at all." As usual, he is understating the case. He and his family suffered unbelievable hardship until they finally were permitted to go out in 1943 on the second trip of the *Gripsholm*. At that point he had no way of knowing what had happened to all the O.M.S. missions and schools he and his co-workers had labored so hard to create. But he knew that eventually the war would be over, and there would be work for him to do in the Far East. He was determined to go back.

"I settled in Los Angeles after the *Gripsholm* brought us home," Uncle Bud says. "I was there for five years—the longest I'd been home since 1909." What he does not say is that he spent those five years speaking everywhere he could, telling about the work that had been done, mustering support for the work he hoped to do. By then, the third generation of Kilbournes—Ernest, Elmer, and Edwin W.—were coming along, and they too had heard the call.

Uncle Bud went back to Korea in 1948. By then he had become Far Eastern director for the organization his father and

Cowman had founded. He was in charge of work in Japan, Korea, China, Formosa, and Hong Kong, and he kept in close touch with the O.M.S. activities in India, Greece, Ecuador, Colombia, Argentina, Brazil, and the Holy Land.

When the Korean War broke out, Uncle Bud and his family were in their compound in Seoul. "We weren't worried," he said. "We had been told the South Korean Army was very strong and would hold out."

At midnight, June 27, 1950, word came that the Kilbournes had better get out. Uncle Bud, as usual, decided to stay. "The women came down at three A.M.," he says, "carrying what they could in their hands. They were taken by truck to Inchon and put on a freighter. It took them three days to get to Japan on that boat, by the way. We weren't worried. We waved good-by to them and told them we would see them back in a couple of weeks. At 6:30 A.M. we got back to our compound, so tired we went to sleep with our clothes on. At seven a Korean knocked at our door and told us the city had fallen. So we went out with what we could carry, got in a convoy, and went to the airport. Communist planes strafed us. As we went out, the army plane we were on was attacked by enemy planes." He paused. "It wouldn't be truthful to say that we weren't afraid, but to tell the truth I was more worried about my family and the boys' wives than I was about myself."

Uncle Bud and the rest of the missionary refugees were put first in an American army camp in Japan, then evacuated (to make room for female refugees) to a camp near Osaka. "Soon after we went to the second camp, they tried to ship us home," he says. "They thought they were doing us a favor. I said, 'Home? I've got a home in Tokyo.' They finally released us." It took him three days to find his wife, and nearly a week before he could get her out of the camp in which she had been placed.

After three months, the UN forces recaptured Seoul. Uncle Bud was the first missionary back into the city. He went at once to his compound and found that the south sides of all buildings had been bombed and shelled away, but the frameworks still were standing. There were tanks and mobile guns sitting in the yard. Some native pastors were living in the ruins of the O.M.S. church, continuing to hold their morning prayer meetings as they always had. Uncle Bud got in touch with a Korean contractor he knew and began cleaning up and rebuilding. He sent for his son Ed, who was in Japan, and the two of them tried to put O.M.S. operations back on a prewar basis. But after three months the Communists were back in Seoul, and they had to run for their lives again. This time, Uncle Bud retreated to Formosa, where he began working on an O.M.S. program for that island. When the Korean War finally was over, he went home to Korea and remained there until his retirement.

O.M.S. is stronger in Korea than in any other country. Approximately 113,000 members belong to O.M.S.-founded churches. "We administer the schools, but once the churches are started, we pull out," Uncle Bud says. "Our idea is to get them self-supporting and then let the people do their own work from there on. But we do keep our schools under our control. Actually, I feel ashamed that I can't be as active as I used to be. I'm now acting only in a kind of supervisory capacity—the boys, all of them ordained Methodist ministers, are doing the real work. If you want a good story, you ought to talk to them. What is there to write about me, anyhow?"

JANUARY 25 § SEOUL

Bob preaches this morning in the South Korean Army Headquarters Chapel. This is the church President Syngman Rhee attends, and he is to be present at the services. Reinhold and I sit near the rear of the church, waiting for the old man's entrance—but, to our surprise, he comes in through a side door, accompanied by General Sun Yup Paik and a number of other high government officials. Even at this distance, he is a commanding, if rather small, figure: his posture is erect, and his face wears a look of quiet authority. Strangely enough, he does not seem to be guarded. He walks slowly to his pew, and when he sits, the entire congregation sits. The choir begins to sing at once. It is superb—as good as any I ever have heard in the United States, even though the Koreans have one less tone in their scale. ("When they come to that note, they ignore it and hold the one before," Bob says.) After the first hymn, a young man in an army uniform sitting a few rows ahead of me suddenly stands up and releases a torrent of Korean. At first I think he is a disturbed man who has gone to pieces, so impassioned are his outcries. Then I realize that he is praying. The second he sits down, in another part of the church another man stands up, and his bellows resound through the auditorium. Then another, and a fourth. Later, when we ask Bob about this, he says, "That's just the Korean style of praying. When any member of the congregation has something he wants to say to the Lord, he stands up and says it. Everybody waits until he's got it all said, and then somebody else says what's in his heart. When these Koreans pray, they really put all their emotions into it."

Bob's sermon, preached through an interpreter, is brief and simple—but although it is couched in terms a child could understand, it is neither patronizing nor condescending. The congregation is rapt, and I sense a ripple of disappointment when he sits down. The Koreans, I learn, like their sermons long. "Once," Bob says, "the Reverend Dick Halverson, of our board, preached a sermon that lasted only forty-five minutes. They all just sat there for a while, and then they sang a song and asked him if he was rested, and then they explained to him that they were waiting for the second part of his sermon. So Dick stood up and preached another one."

After the services, Bob confers with a group of army chaplains who have come along with General Paik. "We're setting up a chaplains' conference for next October," he tells me as we are driving back to the compound. "There are just over three hundred chaplains in the Korean armed forces, and we'll run a four-day program for them—kind of a spiritual regeneration course, plus some exegesis and instruction. Also, while we were discussing the conference, they managed to slip in the idea that they'd like a chaplains' retreat center to be built and used the year around. I ought to try and see if we can't find some way to get it for them." He closes his eyes. As usual, he is asking forgiveness for not doing more.

As we leave Seoul, every pastor in Korea appears to have turned up at the airport to see us off. The crowd is five times the size of the one that welcomed us. Again we are draped with flowers, and again our hands are weak from clasping those of our well-wishers. Bob makes a short speech of thanks and prays, and then we are into the aircraft and off. The crowd is still waving as we leave the ground.

Bob asks me if I am finding enough material. I nod. My head is so full of what I have seen I keep wondering if I will ever be able to get it down on paper. Also, I am all but worn out. "I don't know how you keep going, Bob. I'm not sure I could. I couldn't take a constant diet of these things. All that hopelessness—the icehouse people, for example."

Bob says, "Everything I have, I would gamble on this being true: I believe I have eternal life, and that nothing happens to the child of God by accident. I believe Romans 8:28: 'All things work together for good to them that love God, to them who are the called according to His purpose.' The greatest tragedy is not in suffering, but in suffering for no purpose. That's why I go on. That's why it's worth while to help those icehouse people, even though the help may be only temporary. By helping them, I believe we demonstrated the love of Christ, which must triumph even in the face of hopelessness. I guess that's what keeps me going on."

JANUARY 28 § TOKYO

After breakfast, Bob brings in the Reverend Joe Gooden, the man he spoke to on the telephone just after we arrived in Tokyo the first time. Gooden is making arrangements for World Vision's forthcoming Osaka Evangelistic Crusade. He is a short, neat, bespectacled man who wears a trim Vandyke. He and Bob are old friends. Originally from Texas,

Gooden has been in Japan for more than five years. He and Bob first met when Bob preached one Sunday in the Tokyo headquarters chapel of the army chaplains. Bob hired him for the Osaka campaign because he knows the country, speaks the language fluently, and has a good organizational head. He tells us that the Osaka Crusade will run from May 12 to June 1.

"Wait," I interrupt. "Why did you choose Osaka? Why not Tokyo?"

"For one thing, we want to start out on a fairly small scale," Bob says. "Then, if it's God's design, we'll try another campaign—maybe in Tokyo, if He gives us the word."

"They have a very active Christian Center in Osaka," Joe says. "Each Monday morning there's a prayer meeting. They sing, then people get up and give their testimony. In twenty minutes you might hear from between twenty and twenty-five people. The atmosphere there is very favorable for a Crusade of this kind."

It seems to me I remember hearing that Billy Graham once conducted a Crusade in Tokyo, and I ask Bob if that is true.

"Not a Crusade. He was in for one night. Did very well. Huge crowd."

"Nothing like this has ever been tried before in Japan," Joe says. "We've hired Festival Hall, the finest concert hall in Japan. It seats four thousand. We'll have a selected choir of five hundred voices. The Kyoto Municipal Philharmonic Orchestra will play. This is the first time in the history of the Christian Church in Japan that anything on this scale has been tried. Every major denomination will be represented—we've had the assurances of all that they're going along with us. Bishop Yashiro of the Anglican Church, one of the most prominent Christian leaders in Japan, is helping us organize.

The Christian ministers here never have cooperated in any kind of joint evangelistic movement . . . some of them were in our pastors' conference last year, but not all. Christians have been at work in Japan for a hundred years—this is the centenary year—but in that time they haven't made much impact on the population at large. Less than one-half of one per cent of the people of Japan have accepted Christ. Well, we hope with this Crusade we'll show that Japan is receptive to Christianity." He paused for breath. "It's going to be something, all right. Bob will preach every night. We're planning twenty banquets for businessmen. They'll be addressed by Bob and members of the team. Other teams will go out into the factories and the schools and the stores to preach and pass out literature and make contacts. We'll have meetings for pastors. Then, Bob plans to keep the Osaka office open for six months after the meetings, for follow-ups, to make sure that the people who make decisions can find their way into churches and in turn go out and help us find others."

"Pray the Lord bless us," says Bob.

"Yes," Joe says, "we must pray. Pray and work."

In the evening, we go to a dinner Joe has arranged for a number of important businessmen and government leaders from whom he is hoping to elicit support for the Osaka Crusade. Included in the party are two men, both members of the Diet and each a one-time Cabinet member, who are as far apart politically as it is possible to get in Japan. To complicate matters further, neither speaks English. Nor do most of the others. However, Joe is backed up by his right-hand man, Mr. Goto, and communication is easier than we expected. There is no sign of tension between the two political rivals. They do not look at or speak directly to each other, but they are too polite to indicate in any way that there are differences between them. To do so would be to insult Bob, their host, and all others at the table.

None of these men was born into a Christian family. One, Tokutaro Kitamura, was born a Buddhist. He tells us how he found Christ: he believes he was "pushed" toward Christianity because his father was such an ardent Buddhist. He could not stand the inhuman approach to life of that religion, he says; as a boy he had been profoundly influenced by reading Tolstoi translated into Japanese. He recalls that one day while a young man he went on a hike up Mount Fuji, his Bible in his pocket. There he happened to read the Eighth Psalm. "I felt a fear, and inner need," he says, "and I decided that I was called to Christ."

Kitamura entered politics in 1945 and has been elected to the Diet five times. He was Transportation Manager in the Katayama Cabinet in 1947 and Finance Minister in the Ashida Cabinet in 1948. Bob asks if being a Christian in a predominantly Buddhist country has handicapped his political career. When the question is translated for him, Kitamura shakes his head emphatically. "He says, 'Not in the slightest,'" Joe translates. "He says he keeps a positive view. Nor does he make a secret of the fact that he is a Christian. When his party is out of power, he goes out into the villages and evangelizes."

"What troubles me most is what to preach at Osaka," Bob says. "Have they any ideas on what approach I ought to take?"

Joe polls the members of the meeting, and when he is finished he says, "They say, preach the straight simple message of the gospel. Don't hesitate. Be forthright. Tell your own experience—tell how you were saved. As Kitamura says, 'Keep a positive view.'"

"That's true, I suppose," Bob says. "The gospel is most powerful when it's proclaimed in simplicity. Jesus *is* who He says He is, and does for men what He says He does."

JANUARY 31 § ATAMI

Sensei, as I have come to call Irene Webster-Smith, the lady I met on our first visit to Tokyo, has asked me to come with her to Atami and see one of her pet projects. When we get off the train at this seaside resort, Sensei hires a cab and we set out for the sanitarium, which is about thirty miles south. The road in many places is cut out of a sheer cliffside; far below is the sea, with islands in the distance. The weather is cold, but the sunlight is dazzling. It glints on the silvery fish hanging on racks in the little villages we pass through.

Sensei tells us about the sanitarium as we drive along. "Before the occupation, there were about four hundred barons in Japan," she says. "Then MacArthur did away with the feudal system under which the country always had lived. Among the most prominent of the nobles were Baron and Baroness Kaji, who were Christians. They had a son and a daughter who died of tuberculosis. They also had three younger daughters. These three felt called upon to do something about the disease that had killed their brother and sister. Although education for women was frowned upon by the nobles, they prevailed upon their father to let them go to the University. Makiko-Kao became a doctor. Yoneko became a social worker. The third, Setsuko, also was planning to become a doctor, but she came down with tuberculosis as the others had. When he was stripped of his title and most of his possessions, the Baron had very little left. The two daughters prevailed upon him to take what he had and build a home up in these mountains, overlooking the sea, where the air is fresh and pure and the sun shines steadily. And they said they would operate it as a charity sanitarium.

"The Baron finally agreed. He bought the plot of land which you will see, high on a hill, and some bulldozers came and built a road leading up to it. At the top he built a small frame house. Some Seabees from a nearby naval base helped when they heard what the project was.

"Soon after the house was built, the Baron died. Now the mother and the three sisters are there."

When we get to the site of the sanitarium, we find that the road has been washed out by a recent typhoon. The road looks as though it would be most impossible to negotiate by motor vehicle even if it were in its normal condition: it goes up at an angle of approximately forty-five degrees. We walk up to the small white frame building, and by the time we get there both Reinhold and I are winded. Neither Bob nor Sensei appears in the least fatigued.

The two daughters, Makiko-Kao and Yoneko, are waiting for us on the porch. They are slight, pretty, and they smile as we approach. Over to one side of the small house are cement-block foundations. "Bob is helping us build a small chapel here," Sensei says. "It also will double as a place for the teachers to sleep. Everybody's doubled up here now, the space is so restricted."

The Kaji sisters take us inside, into one of the wards. It is a light, airy room, and seems all the livelier because of the chil-

dren frolicking in it. They are all over the place, tumbling
from bed to bed, laughing and chattering.

"We have twenty-seven children here now," Makiko-Kao
says. "Some are orphans, and nearly all of them come from
very poor homes."

"How are they supported?" Reinhold asks.

"Well, there is a very small government allowance for each
one . . . but not enough to cover the real cost. World Vision
is now supporting eleven of the children. The Lutheran
church helps us a little. But it is very hard. . . ."

"How big is your staff?" Bob asks.

"We have nine—including the nurses, the X-ray technician,
and the laboratory technician. And two teachers to help with
the schooling. You see, we expect that most of our patients
will be cured and go home eventually, and so it is necessary to
keep up with their schooling. But not all will be. . . ."

Her eyes stray to one bed, where a child lies in a cast.

"She has tuberculosis of the spine," Makiko-Kao whispers.
The child, seeing us looking at her, tries to smile.

We proceed to another ward, where there is even more ac-
tion than before.

"These children are the happiest we've seen anywhere on
this trip," Reinhold says.

Bob says, "It bothers me that we're supporting only eleven
of the children, Sensei. We ought to be supporting them all.
Or the staff. We can't just support part of a project. My
board won't stand for that."

We go in to see the bedridden sister in a tiny cubicle where
she has been lying since the sanitarium was built. She is as
cheerful as her sisters. Bob prays with her. "O Lord," he says,
"help these good women in their work." On the way back to
Atami in the car, he says, "Think of those girls and

their mother. Once they were members of the ruling class . . . now they are ruled only by the idea of service to the Lord."

FEBRUARY 2 § TAIPEH

My first sight of the island of Formosa, which its inhabitants call Taiwan, startles me pleasantly. It is as verdant as Ireland. Somehow I had expected it to be brown-gray, like Japan and Korea, perhaps because of the incessant tales of the sufferings of the millions of refugees Chiang Kai-shek brought with him when he retreated here from the China mainland. As our plane lands at Taipeh, the capital, I look out the window and see gun emplacements below, manned by uniformed men. I point them out to Bob. "Don't forget, this country is at war," he says.

Lil Dickson, her daughter Marilyn, and Marilyn's husband, Howard Tank, are waiting for us. At first glance, Lil proves to be everything Bob has said she is—friendly, jolly, yet showing vestiges of amazing strength. She shepherds us into her station wagon (a gift from World Vision) and tells us she has worked out three alternative itineraries.

"You just show us what you think Dick ought to see, Lil," Bob says. "It's all up to you."

"We'll keep busy," Lil says.

§ THE LADY KNOWN AS LIL

Before I spent more than a couple of days with Lillian Dickson, I began to realize why, to uncounted thousands of the estimated ten million souls on the island of Formosa, she is a saint—or as near to being a saint as anyone they ever have met or ever expect to meet. Lil Dickson does not look like a saint. She has none of those ascetic, sensitive features one sees in pictures of saints. She looks more like the chairlady of the Cake Committee for an Epworth League covered-dish social. She is five feet tall, inclined to rotundity, and has a broad face and a wide, toothy smile. A Presbyterian of the Canadian branch of the church, she is the wife of Jim Dickson, a missionary. For about two thirds of her married life she lived as most missionaries' wives do. She raised two children and sat around looking sweetly capable or capably sweet, enduring the hardships of life in the bush. Then, almost overnight, she got busy. Wearing a knitted sweater over a faded print house dress, carrying a battered brown bag that rats gnawed one night while she was sleeping in a native hut, Lil has walked thousands of miles up into the unexplored Formosa mountains, carrying on a one-woman missionary and medical service for the primitive tribes who exist in them.

These mountain tribes—the principal ones are the Ami, the Brun, the Paiwan, and the Tyal, and there are four smaller groups—are as savage as any who live anywhere on earth. Until a generation ago they were head-hunters. One old chief once told Lil proudly that as a young man he had taken more than sixty heads. ("It made me thoughtful," she told me, "but I decided not to think about it.") The Japanese, during their half-century occupation of Formosa, stamped out head-hunting. *They* thought. The habit, once acquired, is hard to break. Chiefs and warriors still vanish mysteriously when there is unrest among the tribes. On one occasion Lil was in danger of losing her own head.

She and some Mennonite missionaries had carried some medicine to a village in which all the people were suffering from worms. As soon as the natives took the drugs they became violently sick. They gathered in a circle, arguing excitedly, casting ominous glances at Lil and her friends, who tried to smile back brightly and began to sing hymns to keep up their courage. "We went to bed that night not certain that we would wake up," Lil says. At dawn she was shaken roughly by the chief's assistant, who explained that several members of the tribe had been in favor of killing the missionaries the night before. "But we decided to wait, and now we are not sick," he said.

The approximately 17,000 natives in the Formosa mountain tribes are of undetermined origin. Since they have no written language, there is no record of where they came from, although according to their handed-down legends they came "out of the sea." Anthropologists, noting their resemblance to Polynesian tribes, believe they might have come from the South Seas. Wherever they came from originally, when they got to Formosa they holed up in the mountains and only ventured down into the plains when provoked into war by other natives who had come over from the China mainland. How they managed to survive over the centuries is a mystery. They always have had an incredibly hard life. Hundreds of them die from disease each year. About one child in every eight reaches the age of twenty-one. They are subject to tuberculosis of lung and bone, to worms, dysentery, leprosy and to diseases of the skin. They are all undernourished, for nothing much will grow in the craggy mountain soil. They have no crafts or skills as their South Seas relatives do. Their only ornaments are the ugly purple tattoos they wear on their faces.

As though all this were not bad enough, the tribes always have been subject to oppression. During this century they first endured the Japanese, who treated them like animals, and later the Nationalist Chinese, who have made their lot little better.

For generations, missionaries had been unable to do anything with these people. For one thing, they were hostile; for another, the Japanese barred the missionaries from the mountains. When Lil Dickson and her husband arrived on Formosa in 1927, fresh from college, they were told that the mountaineers' plight was hopeless. Jim Dickson did not agree. He set about doing what he could, but his other duties—preaching, teaching, setting up schools and clinics and hospitals—did not give him time enough to devote to the aborigines. Nor did Lil do anything about them; she was busy raising her two children, Ronald and Marilyn. Also, her husband's church headquarters in Canada did not believe that missionaries' wives should be anything but wives. In 1940, World War II drove the Dicksons back to America, from where they went to work in British Guiana for five years. As soon as hostilities ceased in 1945, Jim tore back to Formosa. Lil joined him a year later. By then her children were grown and in school in the United States. Jim was still chafing over his inability to do more, and that was when Lil began trudging up into the mountains.

Lil has been walking for thirteen years, venturing into situations that would make many men hesitate. Carrying her accordion (she learned to play when she was forty-six, so she would have some way of bringing music to the tribes) and the rat-gnawed suitcase, which contains mainly an assortment of medicine with a change of underwear tucked into one corner, she became a familiar—and welcome—figure in parts of Formosa where no other white person had ever been seen.

She has been in danger of losing her life so many times that she cannot recall them all. She has been horribly sick with dysentery and with skin infections picked up from eating native food fertilized with night soil and from sleeping in filthy native shelters. These experiences have given her a somewhat optimistic view of life, best exemplified by a time when, after a three-day journey to a mountain village, she found to her delight that the natives had set up a bath for her. "Imagine," she cried, "a *bath*—here!" It was not until she had begun to soap herself that she realized that she was bathing in a pigpen.

This bath came at the end of a trip that was in some ways one of the worst Lil ever made. One autumn a few years ago Jim asked her to go to the village of Mikasa ("All my adventures usually start with Jim asking me to go somewhere," she says). Lil asked another missionary wife, Eugenie McMillan, to go along with her for company. They first went by train to Hwalien, a little city on the east coast, where they bought some supplies preparatory to going up into the mountains. When they left Hwalien it was raining, but not hard. By the time they got to the village of Giok-li, all the rice fields were flooded, the rain was coming down fiercely, and the wind was high. There was not a soul on the streets; everybody had gone into the huts to wait for the typhoon to pass. Lil and Eugenie made their way to an inn that had been built by the Japanese. They shared a bowl of soggy rice and, still in their soaking-wet clothes, settled down for the night.

"Next morning," Lil says, "we were surrounded by water. Most of the houses were flooded. The streets were rivers. Our inn was not flooded, but the water was up to within a couple of inches on the floor. It was like being in an anchored boat."

They could not go out that day. Toward evening, the inn-keeper brought them some news. "People are tying their children to boards and logs, so they can ride out the flood," he said.

"What flood?" Lil asked. "Are you expecting more rain?"

"There is an old dam up in the mountains, holding back a lake. It has not been repaired for twenty years. We're sure it's going to go tonight."

"Let's get out now," Lil said.

"Impossible," the innkeeper said. "The whole town already is surrounded with water." He paused. "One thing— this inn will go fast in a flood."

Lil and her companion looked at each other. They said prayers. Then, still wearing their wet clothes, they settled down and went to sleep. As it turned out, the dam did not break, but the two women were marooned in Giok-li for a week. Lil did not mind. "We got a lot of work done," she says. "There was a native pastor there, and he helped us translate a book about child evangelism into Formosan Chinese."

The natives were saying gloomily that the two women would be stranded for months. All bridges for miles around had been washed out. After a few days some runners came down from the mountain village of Mikasa and said the trail up was passable. Even though she knew that "passable" to a mountaineer meant something less than that to her, Lil followed the messenger back. Before long they came to a railroad bridge where all the understructure had been washed away. Only the rails and ties remained, sagging down like a limp clothesline. Hundreds of feet below was a rushing river. Lil and her companions breathed prayers and set out. Somehow they got across, only to be confronted a few miles farther on by a bridge that had been turned over on its side. They had to walk along the upended edge to cross that river. On the other side some mountain folk were watching their progress with interest.

"Either they're praying for us or laying bets," Lil said.

They finally made it across, and after another day and night of walking along precipices and over swinging bridges with thousand-foot drops below, they finally reached Mikasa. That was when they were grateful for the pigpen bath: "And as a matter of fact," Lil says, "I would have been grateful for a tin cup of drinkable water."

That night she slept in a room separated from the pigpen only by a flimsy curtain. Another time, sleeping in a native hut, she awoke to find a goat peering into her face. She has slept under trees and bushes, and on the banks of rivers; by now she is so accustomed to strange beds she does not feel quite right when she is in a comfortable one. In one mountain village the natives gave her a large, spacious Japanese-style house. It showed signs of having been elegant once, and Lil could not understand why the villagers were not using it themselves. She made herself a bed on the floor and went peacefully to sleep. Next morning she asked the chief why such a fine large house was unoccupied. "A Japanese committed suicide there," she was told. "The house is haunted."

Living under such conditions so much of the time has toughened Lil. She seems to know no fear. One morning last January she took me up to a village called Pu-li to show me some installations she has helped build there. The mountain road over which we traveled obviously had been scratched along the side of a sheer cliff with a nail file. It was just wide enough for one automobile, and there was nothing to keep us from plunging over the side into ravines at least five hundred feet deep. In addition, the driver was a madman; like all Formosans, he was not satisfied unless he was pressing the accelerator to the floor board. In spots the road was muddy and accordingly slippery, and several times we skidded and lurched treacherously close to the edge. I never before have been so frightened. Throughout the whole hour-long ride, while the sweat streamed off my forehead and ran down inside my clothes, Lil chattered away cheerfully, oblivious to the danger, trying to make me believe that she was unaware of my terror.

She is equally fearless in human relations. Once, while making a survey trip to seventy mountain churches to find out what kind of shape they were in, she heard of a chief who had been persecuting members of his tribe who had become Christians. A native policeman told her that this chief had been in the habit of going with a group in the middle of the night to a new Christian convert, sometimes a widow or an old person, and beating the victim or demanding protection money. Lil was in a village five miles away from the chief's when she heard this report. It was near midnight. "Let's go and see that man," she said.

"He'll be asleep."

"We'll wake him up," Lil said. She made her way to the

village and found the chief lying in his hut, sleeping off a drunk. She shook him violently.

"You've been beating Christians," she said. "I can make big trouble for you. I don't want to do it, but I can. If I hear of just one more instance, I'll get after you."

The chief stared at her for a moment, then dropped his eyes. "I *mean* it," Lil said, again. Then she turned abruptly and left.

The friend who told me this story added, "That chief could have thrown a knife or spear and caught her right in the back. Could have killed her. She knew that. She never looked back. And incidentally, that chief never again caused any trouble."

Such evidences of courage do not mean that, inside, Lil is not tenderhearted to a fault. "Mother never keeps anything if she can give it away," says her daughter Marilyn. One night Lil met an old woman shivering on a train on the way to Hwalien. When she learned that the other had tuberculosis, she took off her own coat and gave it to her—even though the weather was very cold and she knew it would be days before she could get back to Taipeh and buy herself another. She gives blood so often that her family fears for her health. One night in the town of Taitung, she and I were invited to go to a wedding being held by some members of the Pyuma tribe. On the way I remarked that we should have bought something for the bride. Lil poked into her handbag and came up with a brooch. "We'll give her this," she said. The next morning we flew to Ko-ching in a tiny two-motor aircraft designed to carry six people. Thirteen were aboard. The flight was more touch than go, but the pilot handled the plane superbly. On the ground he recognized Lil (everybody, all over Formosa, recognizes Lil) and told her he was a Christian. "I always pray before I take off and before I land that ship," he said. Lil beamed. She dug into her bag and pulled out her most precious possession, a New Testament she had been carrying for years. "I want you to have this," she said.

It is this generosity and Christian concern that have enabled Lil to accomplish, in thirteen years, what scores of missionaries never had been able to do in decades of effort. One thing that always hampered missionaries was the difficulty of communicating with the aborigines. "How can you tell them about God," one said in despair, "when their language has no word for God?" That never stopped Lil. "I always have worked on this theory," she told me: "First you find their need, and fill it—and then you find their real need. Their *spiritual* need." This plan has enabled her to establish and maintain more humanitarian installations than she can remember offhand. One day, as we were bouncing along on the diesel trolley that runs along the east coast from Hwalien to Taitung, Lil gasped out a list of her current projects for me. The recital, plus her stories of the various works, took up three of the five and a half hours required for that agonizing ride.

"First of all, we've set up seven clinics for the mountain people," Lil said. "No, eight: at Chutung, Pu-li, Hwalien, Koan-sam, Giok-li, Taitung, Sin-Khang, and Pingtung. Each of the places gets about one hundred fifty patient-visits every day. Some of them do surgery. All of them we've established in the last three years. Pu-li is our biggest place—we've also got a kindergarten training school for girls who want to be teachers there, and another one at Koan-sam, with about fifty girls in each. At Pu-li we also have a home for handicapped children and one for mentally retarded children. We have a hospital attached to the clinic with beds for about fifty patients. We have a tuberculosis sanitarium, and a children's home for mountain orphans—thirteen that are real orphans, and about ten more who are children of TB patients. Near Sin-Khang we've also set up a children's home for orphans and at Phok-ai we have a home for children of prisoners.

"Now, that's all mountain work. There's some city work, too. There's the leprosarium. . . ."

Lil found the leprosarium outside the Taipeh city limits in 1947. It was a government institution, but the Formosan government in those days, as in these, had its hands full with its international problems. It had left the institution in the hands of an unscrupulous superintendent who was selling most of the food the government sent into the camp. The lepers had one bowl of rice apiece each day. They had to cook the rice in filthy pots and old tin cans, which for many was a terrible ordeal. Lacking fingers and sometimes limbs, they set the pots on the stoves as best they could. Since a characteristic of leprosy is skin anesthesia, the patients often burned themselves horribly as they attempted to lift the hot vessels off the stove. They could not feel the burns, but the festering, running sores added to their misery. They had no beds or chairs. Many of them were blind. All were easy victims of insects and vermin. There were 1000 lepers in the place, waiting to die. A doctor visited them occasionally, but he had no drugs to administer. When Lil first discovered this camp it was averaging three suicides per week.

"Why do so many people kill themselves?" she asked one leper, who had been a schoolteacher.

"Because there is nothing for us," he said. "Nothing new comes into this camp. Nobody visits us. We have nothing to look at or listen to or read. We have nothing new to think about, and so we think about our bodies, and for many of us it is too much."

The lepers were planning a revolt. They had taken as much as they could endure. They were going to kill the superintendent and his three or four helpers as a dramatic gesture to call attention to their plight. "Hold off," Lil begged the leader. "I'll see what I can do." First she took a woman doctor out to the camp and appealed to her to visit the lepers regularly. The doctor was willing but all but dumfounded by the enormity of the task. "Where will I begin?" she asked.

"Begin with the ones nearest Heaven's door," Lil said.

She took every cent she could lay her hands on—she and her family deprived themselves of proper food for weeks—and spent it on drugs with which the doctor could ease the suffering of the patients closest to death. Then she wrote friends in the States, begging them for money to buy medicine for the cases in which there was some hope of recovery. Meanwhile she and a friend set up a kitchen to feed the patients.

The revolt was put off but Lil realized that her own efforts were not enough. Aid on a bigger scale was needed. She approached an official in charge of recommending distribution of American aid appropriations and asked him for money. "Mrs. Dickson, we are not giving this money to charity," he said flatly.

That man later moved on to another assignment. Lil went to his successor and again was turned down. She would not give up. "Look," she said, "out here we're fighting a war of ideologies. The Communists kill lepers. At this colony we're faced with a situation where they're killing themselves because the United States won't help them."

The man still was adamant. Lil nagged him until he agreed to go to the colony and see the lepers. After an hour there he was convinced. He set machinery running to help her get an aid grant. With it she built eight dormitories to replace the shacks and huts the lepers had been living in. Then she raised money to hire people to cook their food. She arranged for a doctor to visit the camp every day and sneaked money out of her husband's salary to pay him. She persuaded two Marburg Mission deaconesses, nurses trained in Germany to do medical missionary work, to make the camp their mission. Having provided temporary relief for the lepers' physical needs, she turned her attention to their "real" needs. She built a chapel. The trouble was, the lepers who had no legs could not attend. Lil had the able-bodied patients build small basketlike carts in which the cripples could be wheeled to services. She laid cement walks all over the camp, all leading toward the chapel, so that the ones who had difficulty walking could get to the services. The lepers were eager to help; they welcomed any chance to do something useful. Lil then proceeded to get them a kiln so that they could set up a brickmaking business. Others she encouraged to cultivate a garden and raise their own food.

Still, there were some who could not work, and many of those could not read the books and magazines Lil was pouring into the camp. It struck her that they could enjoy movies. She went to a U.S. Information Service official and asked if she might be placed on their film-distribution list so that the lepers could see an educational movie once each week. "This is political propaganda work we're doing here," the official said, "and we don't regard lepers as politically important." Lil happened to mention this in a monthly report she writes to people in the United States who send her contributions. One person wrote a furious letter to the U.S.I.S., and shortly afterward the man who had turned Lil down went to her and apologized. The lepers got their movies once a week.

Lil next turned her attention to residual problems. Once the doctor began his work, a few lepers were cured and many cases were arrested. In Formosa, as in Korea (and throughout the Far East generally), the fear of leprosy is so ingrained that cured cases cannot return to the villages from which they originally were driven. She set up two houses in which cured patients could live and work. There also was the problem of lepers' children. Leprosy is not hereditary, but small children are most susceptible to it; the virus gets into their bodies and may lie dormant for years before erupting. Lil persuaded leprous mothers to give up their babies, and built two homes for children born to couples in the camp.

If Lil is unrelenting in her efforts to help the needy, she is equally strenuous in her campaign to convert them to Christianity. She has had great success in the leprosarium, but she likes to tell of a man who stubbornly resisted her. "He was in a room with five others," she says, "and I'd helped lead all of them to Christ. This man was a devout Buddhist. I couldn't do anything with him. For two years I prayed for that man, and finally I lost my patience. I said to him, 'Look here—everybody in this room is a Christian but you. When we all get to Heaven, we're certainly going to miss you.' It worked. He didn't want to part from his friends. The next time there was a baptism, he came."

Lil told me she visits the leprosarium (which the patients have named Lok-Seng-I, or Happy Life) once a week when she is not going through the mountains. She also has a number of other urban projects in Taipeh—two homes for boys who formerly were in prison; two homes for boys who graduate from the first homes and either go on with their studies or go to work; and the Mercy's Door Clinic for the poor, which gets 175 patient-visits every day. She sends a minister regularly to visit the city's jails, and she herself goes to the Women's Prison once each week. On Sunday afternoons she conducts outdoor services for pedestrians on the streets. She also has set up an evangelistic church in a building right on the edge of the street known as Sin Alley, where the roughest saloons in Taipeh are located. All year round she distributes clothes to the needy which are sent to her from the U.S.

Lil's energy is such that it is hard for her friends to realize that she passed her fifty-ninth birthday last January 29. She was born Lillian Le Vesconte in 1900, daughter of an immigrant from the Channel island of Jersey who operated a flour and feed mill near Prior Lake, Minnesota, about thirty miles south of the Twin Cities. Lil attended public schools in Prior Lake, went to St. Paul to high school, then matriculated at Macalester College in the same city. There she met a tall, gaunt young man from Dalzell, South Dakota, Jim Dickson, who was planning to go on to Presbyterian Seminary at Princeton and then to enter the mission field. They fell in love at once and planned to marry as soon as Jim was out of school.

Unexpectedly the youngsters encountered opposition from Lil's employer, Dr. Glenn Clark, a professor who later was to become famous as a writer on religious subjects. Lil was working her way through Macalester by acting as his secretary. Clark was the prototype of the absent-minded professor, and his handwriting was all but indecipherable; once a student brought him a test paper and asked him to translate the comment he had written while correcting it. Clark screwed up his brow and stared at the paper for five minutes. Then he said, in triumph, "It says, 'Please write more legibly.'" One day Clark dumped two handfuls of odd notes, written on the backs of envelopes and paper bags and other scraps of paper, on Lil's desk. "I can't make out any of these things," he said. "Maybe you can, and if you can, put them in order. It's an article I'm writing." Lil set to work and presently managed to type the notes into the form of an article, which Clark called "The Soul's Sincere Desire" and sold to *The Atlantic Monthly*. This convinced him that Lil was indispensable. He implored her not to get married, but Lil had made up her mind. As soon as Jim was ordained a minister, the Canadian Presbyterian Church asked him to go to Formosa; he and Lil got married and set out. Except for the World War II years in British Guiana and a couple of one-year furloughs, they have been there ever since.

"My work is peanuts compared to Jim's." Lil often says. In one sense that is true, for Jim Dickson has gone about his mission in an orderly manner, looking to the long view, educating and converting natives who in turn go out and educate and convert others. But as Jim points out proudly, Lil began her work without the backing of any organized church or charitable institution: "She saw the need, and hoped God would help her meet it."

Lil carries out her program with the assistance of a staff of twelve, some of whom work part time, all of whom are badly underpaid. She refuses to acknowledge that she is the head of the office: "God is the boss here," she says. Each page of her account book is headed *In Account with God*. The book is kept by a former banker, a man who was about to become president of a Taipeh bank when he threw up that career to become a theological student. ("He's in his third year now," Lil says, "and pretty soon he'll be ordained.") God's bank balance is always distressingly low. "We never finish the month with any money on hand," Lil says happily. Five years ago, when she was back in Canada on furlough, the manager of the bank where she does her business called her in for a talk. "Mrs. Dickson," he said, "not long ago I had to put a quarter into your account to keep it open." Lil smiled and handed him a half dollar: "You'd better take this," she said, "because it's going to hit bottom again this month."

Lil's ordinary way of raising funds for her work dismays her friends. She simply writes letters that tell of natives who need help, but she does not actually ask for money. A couple of years ago, her brother, Harold Le Vesconte, an attorney, suggested to her that she might get more contributions if she made herself into a tax-free organization. The idea was repugnant to Lil. She felt that if she incorporated she would spend most of her time attending to financial matters and that her walks into the hills would suffer. Le Vesconte kept after her, and finally she registered her work as The Mustard Seed, Inc.

"What kind of a name is that?" Le Vesconte asked.

"It comes from the Bible," Lil said.

"Nobody will understand what it means," Le Vesconte said.

"They will if they look it up," Lil said.

Le Vesconte looked it up himself. In Matthew 13:31, Jesus says, "The Kingdom of Heaven is like a mustard seed, which a man took, and sowed in his field: which indeed is the least of all seeds; but when it is grown, it is the greatest thing among herbs, and becometh a tree, so that the birds of the air come and lodge in the branches thereof."

If He had been referring directly to Lillian Dickson, comparing her with the mustard seed, He would have been underestimating her.

FEBRUARY 2 § TAIPEH

The leprosarium called Happy Life sits on a hillock amid grounds that have been worked over with loving care. There are flowers everywhere—chrysanthemums, peonies, roses, and poinsettias. The trees are neatly pruned and the bushes are cultivated carefully. "The lepers do all this work themselves," Lil says. "Those who don't work on the grounds help out in the brickyard we've started. The yard already is doing very well. Someday these people might be self-supporting."

We drive up to a parking area near the chapel Lil built. This is the day when the babies are brought over from the separate house Lil has built to be shown to their mothers, and all the lepers in the colony who are parents—and able to get about—have gathered around the little frame church. They smile and wave in greeting as we mount the steps. Many of them are in worse condition than those we saw at Taegu. Yet they smile and welcome us.

"Some of the mothers just can't take it, so they don't come to see their children," Lil says softly. "You know, it takes a good deal of persuasion to get them to give up their babies, and some of them just never get reconciled to it."

We go into the chapel and up onto the platform where the minister customarily stands when preaching. The sight before us might have been painted by some cruel, deranged Picasso: twisted faces, faces with holes where the nose should be, bodies blotched purple and brown with sickly yellow. Nurses bring in the babies. Bob, Lil, and the nurses pick up each one and hold him high. Many of the hideous faces gush tears. One young woman lurches forward, stretching up her handless arms as her baby is shown to her. Slowly her cracked and sunken face folds into love, then sorrow, and she puts the ends of her arms to her eyes and turns and flees down the aisle.

One woman, I notice, seems perfectly healthy; I ask Lil about her.

"She's married to a leprous soldier," Lil says. "She won't leave him. She can't live here because she hasn't got it herself. And we convinced her that she'd better give her baby to the baby home. So she comes here on the seeing-day and looks at it and visits with her husband. There are several people here, or near here, who don't have leprosy. One woman put her husband in here and went out to work to earn money to help feed him. She gave him the money, then found out that he was using it to gamble with. She tried to commit suicide. We found her and told her we would stop him from gambling, and so she moved into the compound."

As the children are taken away, the lepers sing "God Will Take Care of You."

We go a few yards away to the Crafts House, named after the Reverend Daniel A. Poling, noted clergyman and editor of *Christian Herald*. "There's a story behind this house," Lil says. "Once when I was in the States I went to Dr. Poling and asked him for some money for this colony. He said, 'No, I can't get into leprosy—I've got too many other things demanding my attention.' The next day he called me and said, 'God must have been listening to our conversation. I've just had a legacy of twelve thousand dollars marked for work with lepers. It's yours if you want it.' With that, we built this occupational therapy house and two other buildings."

In the Crafts House is a small display of things made by the lepers—wood carvings, embroidery work, pieces of furniture. Lil picks up an ebony figure of a water buffalo, the beast-of-all-work on Formosa. "The man who did this has no fingers. Yet he still can carve—he ties a hammer to one hand and a chisel to the other."

We go on to the buildings in which the lepers live. They are four to a room; and the rooms are clean and well kept. "What Christ has done for these people is unbelievable," Lil says. "Once hope is born, self-respect sets in. Before, they simply lay in these rooms on the floor. They had nothing to eat with, nothing to cook in. They simply lay in here waiting to die. Now that Christ has come into their hearts, they do as well as they can with what they have. Those who can still move about care for those who can't. The ones" (her voice lowers) "like this." She indicates a man who is little more than a mass of skin-draped bones lying on a bed just inside a doorway. He is deaf, dumb, and blind, and his body is all but eaten away. Lil touches him. A hand falters into the air to signify that he knows someone is near.

"He was a Christian before the disease destroyed his senses," Lil says. "There is still hope there. All he's doing is waiting to die. But he's waiting with hope in his heart."

"Tell about the coffin, Lil," Bob says.

"Some of them came to me, soon after I started working out here," Lil says, "and said that they felt a body simply couldn't be taken into the chapel for a funeral service without a coffin to lie in. I said, 'All right, we'll get a coffin,' and I had a man in the city make me one lined with metal so it could be used over and over. He delivered it one afternoon and set it on the porch of our house. That had to be the day that some officials from the Canadian Presbyterian Church were visiting us. Those people don't exactly approve of my work. They feel a missionary's wife ought to stay home. One of them said to me, 'What's that out on the porch?' And I said, 'That's my coffin.' And they looked at each other. I didn't bother to explain."

She pauses for breath. "That coffin was such a big success that even the Buddhists signed up to use it." She giggles like a schoolgirl; one of the most endearing aspects of Lil Dickson's character is her resiliency. "You know, we're so well organized here now that running this colony is nothing but housekeeping," she says. "You should have seen it before we brought Christ to them, when they were committing suicide. Many a time we were called out here in the middle of the night to talk some poor soul out of it."

We leave the leper camp and go across the road to a group of frame buildings. "We'll just stop here for a minute," Lil says. "This is our Boys Town. Most of these boys were in prison, and I was determined to get them out. You have no idea of the filth in that prison—there was no water in it but an open sewer. First thing, we got them a well. Then I took Bob there and he saw for himself how things were. Boys of five, six, and seven were living with insane men and hardened criminals. The food was terrible, but naturally the men grabbed all of it and the boys took what was left. They were all undernourished and most of them were suffering from one disease or another.

"Bob decided that something had to be done, and he got us this group of buildings. Then I took the Military Advisory Group people to its prison. There was one man in there who was beating boys, and through them I got him out. Gradually we began moving boys out of the prison—but there are still a good many of them in."

The boys in her dwelling are having an exercise period. Some are playing tag, others are working out on the basketball court. All look strong and healthy.

"We're doing our best to build 'em up," Bob says. "But you know, this is only part of our boys' program here. We've also got two second-mile houses in town—places they go when they're finished here. One is for students, the other is for working boys."

"And don't forget the Boys Town Annex," Lil says.

The Annex, a separate colony for the homeless boys, is up the road a few miles. It is situated at the top of a hill, in a forest, and it reminds me of camps I attended as a child. The boys at this project have two horses. They gallop them past us, riding bareback. Inside the buildings, everything is as neat as an army barracks. The boys' bedding is folded back and all the cupboards have been washed and waxed.

"Billy Graham dedicated this place," Bob says. "It was in 1954, I think. Lil, you've done a magnificent job."

"We do what we can," Lil says wistfully, and it is clear her mind is on projects still undone.

We drive back to Taipeh and stop briefly at Lil's office. We meet the bookkeeper who keeps his ledgers *In Account with God.*" Lil throws open the door of a storeroom, in which cardboard boxes are piled to the ceiling. "Christmas cards," she says. "We'll stamp them with a Bible verse and send them out to the villages. Some of the homes they go into have no color at all—and the people get so curious about the bright-colored pieces of paper, they want to know more about the Bible verse."

In another storeroom are bundles of clothes sent Lil by well-wishers in the States. "These are for the aborigines in the mountains," she says. "Imagine trying to dress two hundred thousand aborigines in assorted sizes. Well, somehow it seems impossible—but we try to do it anyhow." She laughs. "Mr. Hamilton, a missionary friend of ours, went out with my husband one day to distribute clothes. It was hot work, and he took off his overcoat. When they were all finished passing out the clothes, Mr. Hamilton found he'd given his own coat away. We gave him one out of the next bundle that came from the States. It's the mountain people we try to help as much as we can. When you see them, you'll see why. Lepers are fairly common in the Far East—and the government does do something to help them. But they do practically nothing for the tribes in the mountains." Again Lil's infectious laugh shakes her rotund body. "One day I heard our little girl singing, 'My country, 'tis of thee, Sweet land of leprosy. . . .' "

"Tell about the child," Bob says.

"We have an eight-year-old girl, adopted," Lil says. "She was found on the doorstep of an orphanage. They had their hands full. There'd been five to seven babies dying each week in that home. So Jim and I took her to our place, and after she'd been there for a while Jim said, 'Why not keep her at home?' We tried to find her mother and couldn't, so we've adopted her legally. That was at the time when all the mainlanders were coming over here. Children were being abandoned by the thousands. Every little village was swarming with them . . . and there was no one to take care of them."

"No one but people like Lil," Bob says quietly.

"Taking care of one child isn't anything," Lil says.

FEBRUARY 3 § HWALIEN

Lil Dickson has brought us down to this city to see her tuberculosis sanitarium. It is a cement-block building approximately thirty feet long by twenty wide without panes in its windows—but with a bright red hibiscus plant set in each opening. Off to one side is an oil drum in which the patients' clothes are boiled. Turkeys and chickens wander about. In the clearing outside the patients squat on their haunches, looking at us half fearfully, half suspiciously. There are twenty of them, men and women, few of them over fifty, but all so wizened and ravaged by tuberculosis that they look much older. The women have inch-thick, greenish-purple strips tattooed in the center of their foreheads. Married women are tattooed with masks across their mouths from ear to ear. The men are marked with a series of small dots beneath their lower lips. These are members of the Tyal. "When we came here, they were known as the fiercest tribe of aborigines on the island," Lil says. "That was in 1927, and they still were taking heads. The Japanese were in control here then, and even they were afraid of them. They wouldn't let us go among them to work. But then, somehow, two of them heard the gospel and came down out of the mountains, and they found their way to our house. They could have been imprisoned, possibly even killed, by the Japanese if they had been caught. We hid them in our basement for a time and taught them what we could— and they went back to their people, those two, and started an underground Christian movement that cleared the way for my going in there."

The Tyal men and women continue to stare at us, as though wondering why we have come.

Lil introduces us to Dr. Ka, the doctor in charge of this project. The doctor, a husky young Chinese, only a few years out of medical school, speaks enthusiastically of his program to stamp out tuberculosis among the mountain people. "We have units up in the mountains taking chest plates and sputum tests," he says. "As of the present time we are treating three hundred patients in their own villages. If we had the man-power and the equipment—and the money—we could elim-inate this disease in ten years' time."

"Manpower is the problem," Lil says. "We haven't even been able to find a nurse for this place. We have the budget to pay her salary, but we just haven't been able to find some-one to come here."

"We've been a-lookin' too," says the Reverend Edward S. Currie, who has come along with us. Mr. Currie is a missionary of the Presbyterian church in the U.S. (Southern). He has been in Formosa only six years; he and his wife went out to China in 1920, were there for two years under the Commu-nists, and finally fled to Formosa when it became apparent that their work was no longer effective on the mainland. Mr. Currie is nearly seventy, and will retire and return to the States next year, but he is still full of vigor.

"The work here is very new," says Dr. Ka. "This building has only been open about one month. In that time we've tried to teach the people how to take care of themselves—how to eat properly and how to sterilize their clothes. Many of them have 'open' tuberculosis—that is, the contagious kind. Some of them will be cured, however, and go back into the mountains and teach others who are sick how to take care of themselves. And some of them may take the word of Christ back with them."

"It used to be that nearly thirty per cent of the babies born to mountain people never lived to age ten," Lil says. "It's a little better than that now—but the death rate is still awfully high."

We have seen all there is to see at the sanitarium, and start to move away. The Tyal people wave at us solemnly as we move out toward our vehicles.

"I tell you what," Mr. Currie says. "We got a ceremony goin' on out at one of our churches this mornin'. I'm sure these men here, Mr. Steinhorn and Mr. German here, would like to see a native pastor installed."

"Well, Mr. Currie," Bob says tactfully, "we've got so many things to see here, I don't know—"

"Only take but a minute," Mr. Currie says. He turns to me and hands me a violent dig in the ribs. "You ever ride a motor skitter?"

I confess that I not only have not ridden one, I am not even sure what one is.

"Motor *scooter*, some people call 'em," Mr. Currie says. "*I* call it *skitter* 'cause it goes skitterin' along. Tell you what. You go 'long with me out to this installation ceremony—you can ride on the back an' I'll drive. I sure do want you folks to see how they install a native preacher down here."

Lil, who has many things she wants to show us, looks alarmed.

"It's very kind of you, Mr. Currie," Bob says, "but I'm afraid we've got so many things to do today, we won't be able to. . ."

"All right, then," Mr. Currie says, swallowing his disappointment bravely. "Tell you what—come on over to my house, then, and set a spell."

We go over to Mr. Currie's house and set a spell. Outside the kitchen door, a vicious-looking baboon is tethered to a pole. "He belongs to the cook," Mr. Currie says. He shows us some snapshots taken when he and his wife were in China, and then he shows us a picture of the place in Virginia where he was born. Soon it is time to go.

"We'd like to stay longer, Mr. Currie," Bob says, "but there are so many things I want these men to see, we'd really better hurry along."

"I sure wish you'd come along out and see that native pastor installed," Mr. Currie says.

"We just can't," Bob says.

"Won't take but a minute or two."

"No, not this time," Lil says firmly.

Mr. Currie, obviously disappointed, says, "Well, if you can't, you can't." Then he strides over to an Italian motor scooter parked near his front gate, mounts it proudly, kicks it off and sails off down the road in clouds of dust.

"I wish we could have visited with him a little longer," Bob says. "Missionaries out here—or anywhere, as far as that goes—get starved for companionship. I suppose that's happened to him. He and his dear wife have been out in Asia a long, long time."

A few blocks from Mr. Currie's house is a compound belonging to three deaconesses from the Marburg Mission of Germany, Sister Kuni, Sister Irene, and Sister Maria. They wear uniforms rather like the dresses worn by the Amish women of Pennsylvania: dark blue, with white collars and cuffs. On the doorstep of their house stand two little girls, one

Dr. Howard Moffett of the Presbyterian Hospital was our guide.

Bob offered a prayer for the people who were living in the abandoned icehouse outside Taegu, Korea.

We found nearly two hun-
dred people, thirty or fort
of them children, in th
icehouse. Some were to
weak to stand. One wa
dead.

"Chip in. We've got to help those people," Bob said. We started by buying bundles of underwear in the Taegu market.

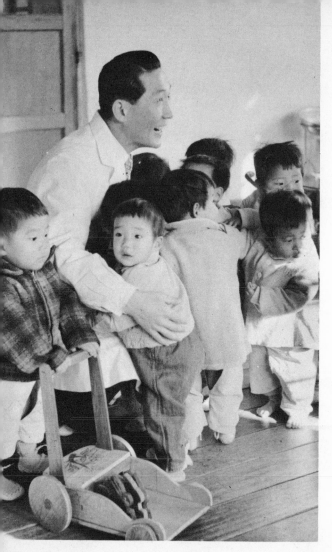

One of the Presbyterian Hospital doctors showed us through a baby home. Most of these babies were found abandoned in the streets of Taegu, some when only a few hours old.

Bob was presented with a scroll attesting to his efforts on behalf of a trade school. Looking on (center) is General Paik, the father, by adoption, of two hundred and forty-one children.

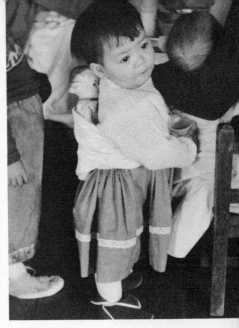

Seoul: a home for children fathered by American soldiers. About the only hope for these outcasts is adoption. World Vision helps to find sponsors for them in the United States.

Hope Boys Town,
Seoul, the mayor at left.

Seoul: Bob listening to the comment of
the oldest graduate of the World Vision
Bible-Study course.

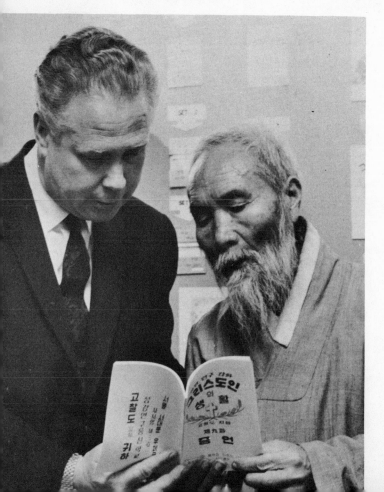

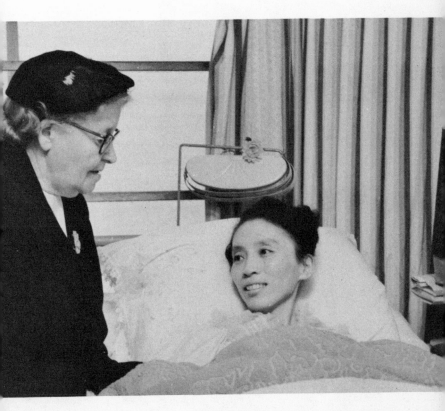

Irene Webster-Smith (''Sensei'') took us to one of her pet projects, the tuberculosis sanitarium at Atami, Japan. Here she talks with Setsuko Kaji, daughter of the institution's titled founder.

Waiting her turn to see h[er]
leprous mother.

Lillian Dickson's Hap[py]
Life leprosarium, Taipe[i]
Formosa. The diseas[ed]
mothers are waiting f[or]
their periodic glimpse [of]
their healthy children.

船音福光恩

Miss Ethel Groce and a native pastor aboard the **Gracious Light** in Hong Kong harbor. Serving God, Miss Groce has spent most of her adult life aboard one boat or another in Chinese waters.

Miss Annie Skau, in charge of the Rennie's Mill Church Clinic, Hong Kong.

The more fortunate Chinese refugees live in these H-block houses in Hong Kong. The less fortunate live in the streets or on the roofs.

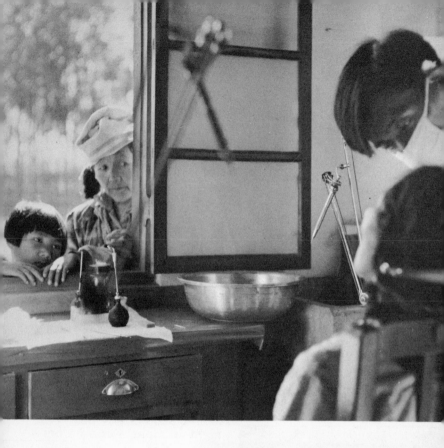

Clinic at Pu-Li, Formosa.

Lil Dickson at another of her clinics, near Kaohsiung. Lil is the closest thing to a saint that uncounted thousands of Formosans ever expect to meet.

Woman and child in their rooftop home, Hong Kong. In the back
ground: their bed.

Mrs. Vyvyan Donnithorne, a worker in the Oriental Missionary Society's Rooftop Program. There are so many children they attend the rooftop schools in shifts.

Some of the 90,000 refugees who live on the roofs give us their smiles on Chinese New Year's morning.

A woman waits for the ashes of a relative at a Calcutta burning place.

At Mar Thoma Church, Malabar, Bob and Bishop Athanasius chat with a girl whom Bob sent to school in the United States.

Bob preaches at the annual Maramon Convention. Despite the withering heat, the service lasted two and a half hours.

Visiting the hospital and old people's home in Kottayam, Bob prays with the doctor, his wife, and his assistant. Through Bob's efforts, the doctor received his medical training in the United States.

Indian beggar, age five. Having no hands, she picked up our coins with her lips.

The riverbed setting of the Maramon Convention.

blind, one a hunchback, with bouquets of rosebuds. They sing a song of welcome, and we go inside.

"I first met the Sisters of this order in Kunming, China," Bob tells me. "They had a home for children they'd rescued from slavery, a midwifery, a dispensary, and a dentist's office. Oh, and a blind school like the one they're running here."

"Here we run a dentist's office, too," says Sister Irene, a tall, stout lady. "Sister Kuni is our dentist."

Bob's thoughts are still in China. "You know," he says, "it was partly because of what I saw these Sisters doing in China that I first started my work. When I first got to Kunming in 1947, Beth Albert, a missionary, met me in a jeep and took me to the house of a woman named Bea Van Meter. That was my introduction to leprosy work. Then she said, 'You ought to go and see the German Sisters and their school for blind children.' We went to see it. The Sisters were doing a wonderful job, but they needed help. Beth asked me if I could do anything for them. I said, 'No, it's too big—they have fifty-two children there, and there isn't any way I can help support them.' But I was terribly ill at ease from that point on. I kept hearing a voice saying, 'If those good women can do something, why can't you?' A month later I was in Amoy, in a mission school for girls. There was one child there whose father had thrown her out. The woman put the child in my arms and said, 'What are you going to do about this child?' By then the voice inside me was so strong and persistent I couldn't disregard it. I said, 'All right,' and I took on the responsibility of caring for that one child. You might say that was the real beginning of World Vision."

We go out and see the blind girls at work at their lessons. The entire compound is alive with flowers, and there are small vegetable gardens behind the classroom. Chickens and rabbits are in a pen, fattening.

"We have three lepers working here," Lil whispers. "They're cured, but they can't go back to their villages. They couldn't even stay here if the townspeople knew they are lepers. There's nothing the matter with them—the disease is long since out of their bodies. So, since they have no place they can go, they work here. They do all this gardening."

"We have twenty blind and one handicapped girl," Sister Kuni says. "She isn't a girl—she was married before she came here. One day she was out gathering firewood when a snake bit her on the leg. Someone tied off her leg below the knee to keep the poison out of her system, and after a month it dropped off. Her husband didn't like her any more, and drove her out. We took her in here, and now she is eyes for the blind girls."

Out in the parking area there is a loud series of explosions and the sound of a motor gunning. Mr. Currie has returned.

"Say, are you folks sure you don't have time to go out and see that native pastor installed?" he calls to us.

"Come and join us, Mr. Currie," Bob says. "We're going out to see an Ami village."

"I believe I'll do that," Mr. Currie says. "I'll just go and put my motor skitter here away, and then I'll come back and join up with you. Then maybe we'll have time to go out and see. . . ." He gives his scooter the gun and tears off.

Bob leads the Sisters in a prayer, and we say good-by to them. We drive about fifteen miles across rice paddies and cultivated fields to the Ami village. The houses are made of bamboo with thatched roofs. The largest structure is a church that sits at one end; it is a building big enough to accommodate a hundred people on the rude benches on the dirt floor. As

ve arrive, scores of children appear in the streets and run to-
vard us. They are good-looking, healthy children, for the
nost part. Bob buys some candy from the village store and
ives it to a man to distribute to the kids, and they all line up
o that Reinhold can photograph them.

"These Ami," says Lil, "are a kind of halfway people be-
ween the native Formosans and the real aborigines who
ve in the mountains. They're the best-looking, the best sing-
rs, and the best dancers of all the tribespeople. There are
nore Christians among them than there are in any other
group. The pastor in this village was a Christian long before
World War II."

We leave with the Ami villagers waving to us, and go a few
niles to another village. This one is not as well kept; buffalo
lung litters the streets, the houses are dilapidated, and the
church is not in good repair. "The minister who was here
lied," Lil says. "We've been trying to get another one to
come in."

"You think you all are going to have time to go over and
see that pastor bein' installed?" Mr. Currie says. "If not, I
better be gettin' along."

"We're due over at the Mennonite Hospital right now," Lil
says.

Mr. Currie and Bob get in one automobile, and Lil, Reinhold, and I ride in the other. Halfway to the Mennonite Hospital Bob's car stops at a crossroads. Mr. Currie gets out,
waves, and begins trudging across a field. He is a lonely figure
against the gray horizon, and I find myself wishing that we
had had time to go and see his pastor installed.

Our driver turns the car abruptly into a side road; a few
minutes later, we realize we have lost Bob and his driver.
"His man knows where we're going," Lil says. When we

finally arrive at the Mennonite Hospital and go inside, w
hear Bob's voice echoing through the lobby. He is on th
telephone, and at first I think he is talking to someon
in Taipeh. Then, with a shock, I realize he is on a trans
oceanic call, speaking with someone in the World Visior
headquarters.

"Strangest thing I ever heard of," he says when he finishe
the call. "I walked in here ten minutes ago, and one of th
doctors said, 'Are you Dr. Pierce? There's been a telephon
call for you from the United States.' It was Ellsworth Culver
in the World Vision office. He didn't even know we wer
supposed to visit this hospital. He just had a feeling we migh
be here."

The Mennonite Hospital is supported by the Mennonit
church of Newton, Kansas, missionaries from which have
been working in this area for about nine years. It has thirty-
five beds. "We're too small to do the kind of surgery that's
most needed here—surgery for tuberculosis-connected
troubles," one doctor says. "There are too many cases like
that. So we do what we can for the TB patients in our outpatient clinic, and try to send the surgical cases somewhere
else. We treat a good many other respiratory diseases, virus
diseases, diseases caused by parasites. This whole island is
infested with worms, you know. Almost everybody has
them."

"Almost everybody throughout Asia has them," Bob says.
"That is, has them in one form or another. It's because they
fertilize their vegetables with human excrement—night soil,
they call it."

On our way to the railroad station, Lil says, "Tuberculosis is a bigger problem than worms. It's more dangerous—
and nobody seems to want to do anything about it. Once I

went to the American Aid people to try and get some money to fight it. The man said, 'Mrs. Dickson, even if we could give you some money it wouldn't do any good—it would be like taking a bucketful of water out of the sea.' I said, 'All right, I'll take my bucketful.' "

"Did they give you any money?" Bob asks.

"No," says Lil. "But I haven't given up. I'm going back and try them again soon."

FEBRUARY 4 § PINGTUNG

We have spent the past twenty-four hours in travel, it seems to me. There being no air service from Hwalien to Taitung, we took the train—a diesel-powered trolley fitted with springless wooden seats that made a 110-mile trip in six hours. During that trip, Lil told me much of her life story. At Taitung we stayed overnight because it seemed the logical thing to do; we are now engaged in a swing down the east coast of the island and up the west, back to Taipei. Jim Dickson appeared briefly in the morning at the hotel in Taitung. He and some fellow missionaries were up from the Pescadores, where they have been working with people who never before have heard the gospel. "We started out from the mainland to the islands the night before last, but a storm drove us back," he told Lil. "I knew there was an odd chance that you and Bob Pierce might be staying here, so we came up." We had time only to shake hands with him—we were due to catch the aircraft for Kaohsiung. Before we left, Jim and Lil stood off to one side, talking quietly. As I watched them from where I was standing, I could almost feel the love radiating back and forth between them. When they said good-by, he kissed her on the cheek and she held quickly to his hand. Then we went to the airstrip.

Now, at Kaohsiung, we have just landed in a field. An old bus is there to take us in to town. When we get there, we are met by Olav and Kari Bjorgas, medical missionaries from the Norwegian Missionary Alliance. Olav, a husky man with a boyish face, graduated from Utrecht University and came here at once; his wife is an occupational therapist who also acts as a nurse in the leprosy clinic they have set up.

"This is a dedicated pair," Bob says quietly to me. "One of the best we're supporting—we're building a facility for them because they really need help. When I first met them, they were living on a salary that amounted to about twenty-five dollars a month. And working their heads off. One night Olav was coming home on his motor scooter when he saw a crowd of people gathered around a girl who had been hit by an automobile. She was dead. She came from a village several miles away from Pingtung. He called a taxi to take the body home, but when the driver saw that the girl was dead he drove off. There was only one thing to do. Olav strapped the body of the girl on his back and took her to her village. There he talked to the girl's family. He told them about his Savior. And today there's a Bible class in the home of those people."

Dr. Bjorgas' clinic is in an old schoolhouse. The panes are gone from the windows, and there are no doors—but to the Bjorgas it is a beautiful building because it enables them to serve.

"When we came down here, the local government said we

were foolish—that we would not find even twenty patients," Olav says. "That was because they did not know about the people who had the disease. Due to the great shame attached to the disease, families of lepers hide them away. Or they hide themselves. We went into the villages and persuaded them to come out." He smiles. "Now that we have shown what we can do, they are coming out of hiding and coming to us of their own volition. We have over three hundred who come to us regularly for treatment now. This city is a harbor—for some reason we do not know, there always are many lepers around a harbor. About sixty per cent of those we have treated, we have managed to arrest."

"How long does the treatment go on?" Bob asks.

"Well, it depends upon the individual cases," Olav says. "Some do not respond for many months. Some must be treated for three or four years. Some cases require surgery . . . that is why we have the three beds in the clinic, for special cases and for those who must stay with us for a time."

Bob says quietly, aside to me, "When we found the Bjorgases, I made arrangements for World Vision to take over the support of the clinic. And I got them a little more pay. Then, when I came back a little later, I found that their own personal living situation hadn't improved at all. They were still living in one dingy room. They took the increase in salary we gave them and bought drugs."

Later he tells me that World Vision is planning to build a hospital for Dr. Bjorgas, similar to the one Dr. Howard Moffett is operating in Taegu.

The Bjorgases take us to lunch in Kaohsiung's one Westernized hotel. There we are joined by Miss Geneva Sayre, a tall, weather-burned lady who looks like one of the pioneer women who first went west to her native Kansas. Miss Sayre tells us that she first went to China in 1921, sent by the Free Methodist Church to Honan Province, about seven hundred miles inland. She stayed there until 1951, and for the last three years of her tour she lived under the Communists. "At first they weren't so bad," she says. "They allowed the people to come to the services and to my house—but then word went out that it wasn't advisable to come any more, and they stopped. They were afraid to come." Miss Sayre was the last missionary to leave Honan, and the last member of her denomination to leave China. Before she left she was imprisoned twice, once for four days of questioning. The second time was the bad one. Some Friends Service Committee relief workers had been traveling through Honan, and she put them up for the night. The police arrived and announced that the travelers' permits were not in order, and hauled them and Miss Sayre off to prison.

"It was a six-by-nine room," Miss Sayre says, "and there we were—a husband and wife and another man and me, two women and two men, in that hole of a room for forty days. It was winter, and very, very cold. Snow came in under the eaves. There was only a bare ground floor, and we had to sleep on that—although on the second night my cook did come with quilts for us, and they let us keep those. They fed us twice a day—rice, mainly, but sometimes steamed bread. They interrogated me all the time—they would take me out for questioning a couple of times each week, trying to get me to say that I was a spy. 'Who are your friends?' they would ask, and I would say, 'All the Chinese are my friends.' " Miss Sayre's voice cracks slightly with amusement and indignation. "One night I had a whole night of it. This officer had me in a narrow room, with two beds in it, and we sat on those beds face to face, our knees touching. There was a single bright light in the room, almost blinding. And there was this very hot fire, which made it worse—after all, I'd been conditioned to the cold in the room where they'd been keeping us. The officer kept asking me where my radio broadcasting station was. He said he knew I was sending information to the enemy. Imagine that. Finally, in the morning, he let me go back to my room." The Communists let her go when the forty days were up, and told her she would have to leave the country. "By then I was glad to go," she says. "I'd had enough of it—and I'd heard of many worse things happening. Three Southern Baptist ministers I knew of were thrown into prison, beaten, and finally given a public trial. The Communists said they had taken money from missionaries who'd already gone out and were giving it to the underground. They tried them in the presence of a huge crowd. The people bit them and hit them and spat in their faces. It was terrible. Later they were thrown into jail again. I never did hear what finally happened to them."

Miss Sayre came to Formosa after she got out of China. Today she and Dr. Bjorgas carry on a medical mission to some of the mountain tribes in this area; she works with the Paiwan and the Bunan, teaching in a Bible school.

After lunch we go to Pingtung, by automobile, where the Bjorgases have set up a children's hospital. "We rented this place from a Chinese family," Dr. Bjorgas says. "And an American, a civilian engineer with the armed forces, heard of what we wanted to do and offered to come in and help us. He pays the rent in return for staying here . . . his heart is big. Most of the children are tuberculosis patients . . . some of them have been with us a long, long time. They will never get well. Their families have thrown them out. Someone must care for them."

From the children's hospital we go on to Pingtung Moun-tain Clinic, a neat little building that services fifty-odd patients per day and has beds for thirty patients.

"I don't know when you get a minute to yourself," Bob says to Dr. Bjorgas. Then, to Lil: "Lil, where does the money for this clinic come from?"

"From God," Lil says, promptly. Then she adds, "The Christian churches cooperate to support this place. It only costs about two hundred thirty dollars a month to run. Most of the people are charity cases."

We go through the clean, bright ward. The patients prop themselves up in the beds and try to smile.

"Look over there," Dr. Bjorgas says quietly, motioning toward an old woman who appears to be wasting away. "She's had an open sore on her leg for twenty years. I found her in the street one day. She'd never known that there was such a thing as a place where she could get treatment. She told me her husband was suffering from heart disease. She brought him in the next day. They are both here now . . . soon they will be strong enough to go home."

He sighs. "But oh, there is so much to be done in this sec-tion. One family we knew about had too many children . . . they could not support them, could not feed them. The father came to me and said, 'Unless we get some sort of help, we must sell our children.' We helped them a little, but it was not enough. It is never enough . . . we can never catch up to the need. . . ."

"We can try," Lil says.

FEBRUARY 5 § **PU-LI**

Lil has been most eager for us to come to this small city, for here is where a major part of the effort to help the mountain tribes is going on. We visit the clinic first—a small brick building, no more than thirty-five feet square. Into its reception room are crammed sixty people on wooden benches, some mothers holding children, many wearing bandages, nearly all with the dumb, helpless look of the being who knows he is sick but does not know what is wrong. Pu-li is in the heart of the mountains. Until Lil Dickson came, these people were all but forgotten. Now the area is buzzing with missionary activity. In addition to this clinic (built by World Vision) there is also a hospital; there are Bible classes and schools for girls who want to be nurses and kindergarten teachers, a home for retarded children, a small tuberculosis hospital for children, and a home for illegitimate children. "Lil has done most of it herself," Bob says.

We went by train from Kaohsiung to Taichung, then took a cab up the mountain to a resort hotel at Sun Moon Lake, a favorite retreat (Lil explains) of Madame Chiang Kai-shek. We were up practically at dawn, and have driven the twenty miles from Sun Moon Lake to Pu-li in time for the services that open every day of treatment at the mountain clinic. Bob is asked to address the patients. He says, "We are hoping not only that you will return to your homes well, but that you will go with the peace of God in your hearts."

The treatments begin. The staff consists of the man every-body calls "Doctor Barney": Bjarne Gislefoss, a Norwegian, and two others, Dr. Sia and Dr. Lo. Dr. Sia is a surgeon; he performs major operations—everything but brain surgery—on a rude wooden table behind a thin partition that separates the "operating room" from the outpatient clinic. Near the operating area, behind a thin cloth curtain, is a postoperative section—a single bed. On it lies a man who is recovering from surgery. "Had cancer of the lymph glands," says Dr. Sia.

Dr. Barney, a tall, slender man with reddish blond hair and clear Scandinavian blue eyes, trained at the Deacons' Medical School Hospital, went into prison relief work, then went to Glasgow, Scotland, to Bible school for two years. After graduating from there he went home for one week and promptly came to Formosa. He has been here ever since, working under the auspices of the Norwegian Missionary Alliance. For a time he worked in the Mackay Hospital in Taipeh, but after two years he felt the call to serve the mountain people, and with Lil Dickson's urging he has come to Pu-li to live and work. "People were walking as many as forty miles to get medical assistance," he says. "One man walked sixty-five miles, and when he got to us he was cough-ing blood."

Dr. Sia, the principal associate, went to medical school in Japan and in the United States, then returned to Formosa to work. Dr. Lo had been in China under the Communists, es-caped, and made his way first to Taipeh and then to this hos-pital, the official name of which is Pu-li Christian Clinic for Aborigines.

The clinic is visited by between two hundred and three hundred patients each day, of whom between ninety and one hundred usually are tubercular. It is Lil's dream to build a real hospital on an eminence a mile away, for the facilities now are inadequate. "This is not good here," Dr. Barney says. "Trucks go by, and the dust comes in while we are operating. And we can do nothing to keep it out." All the facilities are primitive. He has no refrigerator in which to store blood plasma. At present, he is saving a little out of his salary—he earns less than a hundred dollars per month—to buy a small one. However, he does have one piece of fairly new equipment. In the States, Bob appeared on a TV show and told of the work at Pu-li. The officials at a Jewish hospital in Denver saw the show. They had an extra X-ray machine; they crated it and sent it on to Pu-li.

Dr. Barney is doing a job that can only be described as heroic. He puts in a twelve- or fourteen-hour day seven days a week. When he is not seeing people in the clinic, he goes up to the hill (the site that Lil has planned for the new hospital) and treats the inpatients in the bamboo huts that Lil erected. There is a small bamboo church in the hospital compound, hardly more than a thatched roof and a couple of bamboo supports. While Dr. Barney is showing us the hospitals, Lil slips off by herself, goes into the little church, kneels down and prays.

The bamboo hospital consists of ten flimsy buildings. As many as four hundred patients have been in at one time.

"I came up here originally with a Mennonite Medical Mobile Unit," Lil says. "Dr. Sia was on the unit, too. He kept coming back, and kept after me to build a clinic. Finally we got funds together and built this. In 1958, World Vision took over the project. Now they send us eighteen hundred and twenty dollars a month, and that just about covers the treatment of between eight and nine thousand patients—patient-visits, that is."

"This is the only place in which the mountain people can get surgery of any kind," Bob says.

"The trouble is," Dr. Barney says, "often we get them too late. We had yesterday a man who came on the bus from Koehing. He had a hemorrhage and he needed blood. We have no plasma because we have no facilities for keeping it. So we all gave him blood—never mind the type, we did not have time to check for that. With luck, he will pull through. We do what we can. Dr. Sia has done amputations in that little room, skin graftings, lung operations. . . ."

We leave the hospital and drive a few miles out of town to a cemetery. "I just wanted to have a look at this place," Bob says. "I haven't been here for a while, and I wanted to see it again." In a small, quarter-acre plot are rows of headstones. Lil explains it:

"The Taiwanese feel that the mountain people are . . . well, not much better than animals. One day a mountain woman walked into Dr. Barney's clinic with her dying baby in her arms. The baby died as she walked in the door. There was no place to bury it . . . and I learned, to my surprise, that there are no cemeteries in the town areas where the mountain people can put their dead. I sent out a hurry call to Bob, and World Vision sent us the money. Now the aborigines have a place of their own."

Bob leads the group in a prayer. The sun is hot and bright. Wild flowers are growing among the graves, their reds and blues and yellows shining against the simple grayish white stones.

Afterward we go back to Dr. Barney's house for tea. It is over quickly, but not until later do I realize why. Although he was starved for outside talk and wanted to sit with us for a long time, his clinic was pulling him back: he could not bear to be away from it for long, there was so much work to be done.

§ THE WORD FOR "BOOK" IS "TATTOO"

Edvard Torjesen, of The Evangelical Alliance Mission, a Chicago missionary organization that calls itself TEAM, was one of the most patient and dedicated men I met on this trip. Lil introduced me to him in Taichung, whence we had gone from Pu-li, on the afternoon we visited Morrison Academy, an interdenominational school for children of missionaries operated by the members of a number of faiths. Torjesen was an accident, so to speak. While the other missionaries were telling me of their hospitals, clinics, Bible schools, etc., he kept silent, and at first I thought he was either moody or ill. He said nothing about his work. After lunch I sidled over to Lil and asked her about him. "You ought to talk to him," she said. "He's working on the written language for the Ami."

"I thought they had no language," I said.

"They don't," Lil said. "Or—they didn't. That's why you ought to talk to him."

The Morrison missionaries wanted Bob to see a radio station that World Vision was helping to support, and I told him that I would rather stay and hear Torjesen's story. Bob looked disappointed—the first departure from placidity I had seen him permit himself during the trip. It was obvious that he wanted me to have a look at the station, since in his view its broadcasts to Red China were most important. Yet he at once put his personal feelings aside, and when I finally got to talk to Torjesen, I was glad that he had.

Torjesen, a blond man with a massively heavy face, spoke slowly. Like most men involved in highly specialized work, he was reluctant to talk about it to a layman, since mere discussion involved much explanation and translation of technical terms. He began by showing me a chart of the alphabet he had devised. It looked much like our own alphabet, modified for Oriental use. And then he began telling me the story of his work.

"First," he said, "you have to know a little about the Ami." In a few sentences, he sketched in the background.

The legends of the Ami go back to a great flood, as the legends of so many peoples do. "We came from the sea," the old men say, and they tell how all their original ancestors were destroyed in the heavy rains—all but a brother and sister, who floated in a trough used for feeding pigs, and drifted in the flood out to sea. Presently their trough came to rest on a mountain peak. The sister and brother got out, the waters receded, and from them came the tribe. Anthropologists and linguists who have studied the Ami and other primitive tribesmen on Formosa are by now fairly certain that they did come originally from the South Seas, for some of their words bear similarities to those of the Polynesian tribes, and every now and then one of them is born who resembles a Polynesian. But there is no way of comparing their culture patterns through their artifacts for, as mentioned before, these people have no handicrafts. They have been so busy scratching a living out of the barren Formosan mountains, they have had time for nothing else.

The Ami live mainly in the region between Hwalien and Taitung. The two cities are about 110 miles apart, and the Ami live in the country between, in the foothills of the eastern coastal range of mountains. Formosa was ceded to Japan in 1890, and when the Japanese were in control of the island they tried to bring some order into the people's lives. The villages were ruled by councils of elderly men, and those in certain sections operated on a community basis—they hunted and fished together, harvested and planted together. After Formosa was taken over by Nationalist China and Chiang Kai-shek arrived to assume command, little was done for the Ami and the rest of the mountain tribes. The primitives were regarded as inferiors, and when they were not scorned they were ignored. Today most of the civil authority is handled by the police. Not much rule is needed, for although the Ami may have been head-hunters a few generations ago, today they are docile and peaceable. One once said to a missionary, "Why should we fight? Simply living is hard fight enough."

The Ami have become withdrawn and fearful, and accordingly they also have become prejudiced against everything that comes from the outside.

For that reason the burden of Edvard Torjesen has been especially hard. Torjesen arrived in Formosa in 1951. Since then he has been walking into the hills with a pack on his back, visiting all the villages, taking the Word to the people —but communicating only a part of it to them, for his main task has been to invent a written language for them, to translate the Scriptures into it, and to teach them to read it and write it through the use of the Scriptures.

Torjesen learned the language of the Ami by simply pointing at objects and raising his eyebrows questioningly. The
tribesmen would respond, and he would repeat the word over
and over until he was sure of its general meaning. Then he
would write it down in his notebook, phonetically. Torjesen
is a stolid, methodical man; his broad Norwegian face is proof
of that. He was born in 1924 in northern China, of parents
who were in the Norwegian mission there. Educated largely
in China, he went to the United States during World War II
and worked as a civilian with the armed forces. He attended
Trinity Seminary in Minneapolis, Toronto Bible College,
and finally spent one year at the summer Institute of Lin-
guistics in Saskatchewan. Its graduates—more than eight
hundred volunteers, called the Wycliffe band—are working
in both hemispheres, translating the Bible into native languages, and in many cases actually manufacturing languages
for tribes who never had them. The Bible is now translated into around 1000 tongues; according to the Wycliffe
workers, there are 2000 remaining. Thanks to the work of
Torjesen, there soon will be only 1999.

It has been slow work. "I had to work for six months before I could persuade an informant to come with me and go
into the other villages," Torjesen told me. "The Ami had been
trained both by the Japanese and the Chinese to think of their
language as inferior, and they hesitated to help a foreigner
to learn it."

Torjesen had done some linguistic work before, and his
technique was well developed. After finishing his education
he had gone back out to China, and in 1948 had arrived in
Kansu Province in Northwest China, where he had begun
translating the Scriptures into a Mongolian dialect. The war

forced him to leave, but as soon as he escaped to Hong Kong he found a number of Mongol refugees, and they helped him finish his project.

"The way it works is fairly simple to explain," he said on the day we met, "but it is not so simple to do. You go into a place, point at objects, make sounds, listen to the sounds they make, write it down phonetically, and then you analyze the sound system and work out a phonemic alphabet on that basis. You analyze the sounds in terms of the significant contrasts, and you interpret these sounds to make an alphabet based on the sound units. It took me about a year to do that.

"The alphabet worked out consists of twenty-one characters—four vowels and seventeen consonants. Some of the sounds are hard for the uninitiated to say—for instance, they have a fricative *l*—technically, a 'voiceless fricative lateral.'" To demonstrate, he made a whirring sound with his tongue. "And there are other sounds extremely difficult for a foreigner . . . they have *h*s that end words as well as begin them. After an hour of trying to reproduce those sounds so they will be natural to an Ami, I have no mind left."

Working with a pair of native informants, Torjesen first produced a primer setting forth the use of the new alphabet. They began distributing it and teaching from it in the Ami villages, but again ran into opposition.

"The trouble with the primer was that it was designed for illiterates—people who never even thought of reading. They were in the majority, of course. The Ami did not even have a word for *book*—because they had no written language, the concept of any kind of sign and symbol was something they could not grasp. The nearest thing to it was *tattoo*. They do not tattoo their faces, as some of the other tribes do, but they recognized what tattoos—markings—were, and we had to use that word for the written language, and for *book*. Many words thus became portmanteaus.

"Some among them had been to Chinese schools and had learned to read. They were resentful of the childlike simplicity of the primers. So it became apparent almost immediately that we had to give them something more interesting to read in their own language. We decided to pick the book of James to translate first. After we did that, we produced a book of one hundred Scripture passages. Then we got the gospel of Mark published."

Translating the Scripture into terms the Ami could understand proved even more difficult than inventing a word for book. To begin with, the Ami religion, such as it is, is as primitively conceived as the life they lead. They had no word for God. They believe in spirits, good and evil; their religion is a form of animism. It has no name, either.

"We had to study their folklore," Torjesen says. "And that was hard, too, because it is based on superstition and fear, and they did not want to talk about it."

Torjesen spent countless days and nights questioning the old people in the villages, trying to work out concepts which he could put in their terms. As nearly as he could determine, they had conceived of a kind of guardian spirit, which could be likened to the soul, and two other spirits, which were thought of in terms of shadow, or shade. Neither seemed to express adequately the concept of God as Christians know it. Yet it was all Torjesen had to work with. Eventually he learned something of their "medical" practices, and drew inspiration from their use of the word *shade* in the case of sickness.

"When a man became ill, the witch doctor would go into

his hut and lie down on top of him, breathe into his mouth, and chase out the shade. So it seemed reasonable to use the word *spirit*—as it came from the witch doctor—for God. It doesn't make sense to us, perhaps, but it does to them because it goes right back to their original concepts."

Torjesen went on teaching up and down the valleys and foothills. Whenever he could get a man to make a decision for Christ, he gave him a supply of materials and made a teacher of him. There already were some churches in the hills in which the gospel was taught by word of mouth, but today there are more than a hundred churches using the materials Torjesen has provided.

"Right now," Torjesen said as he and I were parting, "we're hoping to finish the Acts by Christmas. Eventually we are going to translate most of the New Testament, which will take many, many years. But of course, as more of them learn the language, there will be more helpers. Eventually we hope to organize schools among these hill people. We hope that by giving them this written language it will contribute to their self-respect and help to make them an asset to the country rather than the liability they now are considered. But, more important to me, we hope it will give them the life that only the message of the Lord can bring."

A friend recently asked Torjesen what he would do when his work with the Ami is finished.

He seemed surprised by the question; the answer was so obvious to him. "Why, I'll just go on and find another people who haven't heard the Word, and help them learn to hear it," he said.

FEBRUARY 5 § TAIPEH

Jim Dickson sits in our room in the Grand Hotel, telling us of the work the church has done on Formosa. Jim's major work here is teaching in the Presbyterian Theological College, established in 1878. "The Presbyterians have been the most active branch of the church on this island," he says. "When I came out they were short of missionaries here, but it's remarkable what they've done. There were about sixty churches in the north and between eighty and one hundred down south, all Presbyterian. There were then two Roman Catholic groups, and a few Holiness churches established by the Oriental Missionary Society. Now, after thirty-odd years, there are over seven hundred Presbyterian churches alone, and at least three hundred Protestant churches of other denominations. At the end of World War II, in Taipeh, there were only fifteen Protestant churches . . . today there are over one hundred. There are three hundred and fifty churches in the aboriginal areas . . . we, perhaps more than any other denomination, have been helping them. Yet there's more, so much more, that could be done." He smiles when we ask him if he plans ever to return to the United States. "I don't believe I'll ever go back," he said quietly. "This is where God wants me to be, here on this island, working with His people who don't know they're His people, helping them find out about Him."

Lil comes bustling in. "Come on, come on, come on, you two," she says. "Your plane leaves in thirty minutes."

We shake hands with Jim and follow her out. At the airport, she literally hurls us through the formalities, spouting the local dialect as though she had been born into it. As soon as we are ready to board the aircraft, she starts to leave. "I saw so many things this trip that need to be done," she says, "I've got to start right away to make arrangements to go up to the mountains again."

I don't suppose I will ever forget the sight of her standing there in the waiting room, wearing her blue cloth house dress, carrying her torn, rat-gnawed bag.

FEBRUARY 7 § HONG KONG

Almost as soon as we are established in our hotel rooms, Bob comes in with his old friend, the Reverend David Morken, in tow. "Dave's going to show us around," he says.

"There's so much to see in Hong Kong, I don't really know where to begin, Bob," Dave Morken says. He is a tall man in his mid-forties, with a quiet, friendly manner, and I take to him at once.

"World Vision's program in Hong Kong isn't very extensive," Bob says, "but even so, there are many things here you ought to see. I want you to see the boat people in the harbor . . . there are more than sixty thousand of them, aren't there, Dave?"

"There may be more, they're coming in so fast from

Red China. Nobody knows how many people are here now —but the government estimates that the population density is about nine times that of Manhattan Island. There may be as many as ten million people here now."

"And only missionaries to look after them, for the most part," Bob says. "The government is doing what it can, but it can only scratch the surface. And the problem here is especially critical, because these people have *no* place to go. This is a dead end. Nowhere on earth are the Lord's workers doing more than they're doing here—and in terms of mass misery, possibly nowhere on earth is the need greater."

While Dave goes downstairs to look after our transportation, Bob tells me something of his background. "When Dave was a young pastor in Lodi, California, he heard the missionary call and went out to Sumatra," Bob says. "He and his wife Helen were caught there in December 1941, when the Japanese overran the island. They fled for their lives in an open boat and finally reached a port where they got on a ship. They spent three months dodging submarines on that vessel. Nobody at home even knew they were alive, and it was a big surprise to their relatives when they finally got back. I met Dave shortly after he got home. We became friends, and then he came into the Youth for Christ movement and we teamed up and went out to China together. That was my first trip. We began holding pastors' conferences in China, and then, while I started to run back and forth to raise money to carry on the work, Dave decided to stay. He was in Shanghai with his wife and three children when it fell to the Communists, and he stayed there eighteen months afterward, under house arrest. Finally they let him go to Japan, and he lived there until 1953, when he came down here because he felt there was a stronger call, more work to be done. Dave isn't a missionary, exactly—he's more of an evangelist than anything else. He serves everybody, all denominations, all over Asia, everywhere that people want to hear the Word. He's preached in Indonesia, Vietnam, the Philippines, India . . . he's always on the go."

Dave returns. "They're downstairs," he says, "Dale McClain and another friend of yours, Bob."

"I was just telling the men about China," Bob says. "Remember those meetings we used to hold up there?"

"Do I remember them?" Dave says. "We used to hold seven or eight meetings a day—in churches, high schools, anywhere we could get a crowd together." He shakes his head. "I couldn't do it today. I don't know where we got all that energy."

We go downstairs, where, to our surprise and delight, Uncle Bud Kilbourne is standing on the sidewalk beside a Volkswagen bus. "Just thought I'd come down to Hong Kong and see how our work here is coming along," he says with a big grin. I tell him I had not realized that the Oriental Missionary Society was active in Hong Kong. "Oh my, yes," he says. "This is one of our most active programs. We'll show you some of our work." He turns to a sturdy, broad-shouldered young man standing near the bus. "This is Dale McClain, our field superintendent, director of the work in Hong Kong."

McClain has a firm, Rotarian handshake and the brisk air of a man who wishes to waste no time in getting the Lord's business done. He reminds me a good deal of Elmer and Ed Kilbourne, Uncle Bud's sons; he appears every bit as zealous and dedicated as they. As the day unfolds I learn that he met the Kilbourne boys in college, became excited about the work they were planning to do in the O.M.S., and decided to follow them out to the Far East. "I was out here before we got chased out of Red China in 1948," he tells me. "Then I went out to India for a while. I realized that we had to have more support from the States, so I went back there—my home is in Akron, Ohio—to try to work with businessmen. I was trying to start a fire in one guy's heart that would ignite it in another's. Well, I did as much of that as I could, and then I decided I had to get back out here. So much work to do. So I went to Korea, and then I came down here."

McClain tells me much of this while we are careering through the Hong Kong streets in the Volkswagen bus. From time to time, as he is making a point, he takes both hands off the wheel to gesture.

"Our men are still traveling all over the United States, trying to arouse people to the needs of the people out here," he says. "We've found that when the ordinary guy hears what the real story is, what the real need is, he goes all out to help. We're trying to crack the plush curtain—trying to arouse people to the genuine needs of others, and to show them that they can serve the Lord by helping to fill those needs."

The Volkswagen narrowly misses hitting a taxi that suddenly materializes out of the dusk, but McClain goes on talking.

"We're taking you out to see our Rooftop Program," he says.

McClain explains that refugees are now streaming into Hong Kong at the rate of approximately 6600 per month, but he adds that that figure may be wrong, because the influx is so great that any statistic may be incorrect at the very instant it is published.

"The Hong Kong government is in a peculiar position,"

he says, "because as you know, the British recognize Red China. Yet something has got to be done with these people who come over the border. So they've begun building huge blocks of apartment houses—H-shaped at the foundation, so they're called H-blocks. Five people are put in each room— that may sound like a lot to you, but it's a good deal better to sleep five to a ten-by-twelve room than it is to sleep in the gutter. About twenty-five hundred people live in each of the H-blocks, and they've put up about seventy-five of them to date. There are nearly one hundred seventy thousand people living in these units now, and they've got about a dozen more under construction. Thirty-seven per cent of the inhabitants of the buildings are children under fourteen. Kids without a future, most of them.

"Something had to be done," McClain goes on. "They were living there in the H-blocks, but they weren't organized— they were running wild. There weren't any school facilities for them. We in the O.M.S. decided we would organize a school for them, and we started in August. We registered three hundred kids and set up schools on the tops of the H-blocks. We had volunteers from various groups that co-operated. We tried to give the children elementary-school education, plus a liberal dose of Bible instruction. We've been leading them to Christ, little by little . . . and those kids will spread the Word to their parents, to other boys and girls. Right now we've got more people wanting to come in than we can handle."

Uncle Bud says quietly, "Every missionary here in Hong Kong is risking his life by working with these refugees."

The statement seems hard to believe. "How so?" I ask.

"We're right on the border," McClain says. "Not all the ones who come across are refugees . . . some are Communists, posing as refugees. If war comes, Hong Kong will fall in a matter of minutes. And we know from the underground that every missionary here is marked . . . there's a Communist assassin just waiting with his name and address. If it comes, they'll get rid of the missionaries first."

McClain turns a corner sharply, and we are at one of the H-blocks. There are six groups of them in the city, he tells me. At first glance the buildings are similar to those low-cost apartment houses the insurance companies have been erecting in New York and other large American cities. At second glance they show themselves to be much more primitively utilitarian. They are nothing but concrete hives, huge Hs when viewed from the sky, with semi-enclosed stairwells and balconies running along the outside. The cross bar of the H contains kitchen and bath facilities on each floor; the uprights are single rooms ranged side by side. Hundreds of lights flicker in the rooms, and as we get out of the bus we immediately are surrounded by buzzing children, each with his hand outstretched and face turned up appealingly. Pushing our way through the small mob, we gain the stairs and, finding our progress blocked by the scores of people rushing up and down, struggle up seven flights to the top of one of the units. McClain shows us the classroom his organization has put there—a screened-in enclosure, furnished with crude wooden benches, a lectern, blackboards, and another screened-in area in which the children play. "I wish there were a class in session now," McClain says. "The principal of this school is a university graduate. A very intelligent man."

We look from our rooftop to the other H-blocks around us. There are people swarming all over the balconies, running from room to room, going in and out, carrying steaming pots from the central kitchens, hanging clothing on the railing to dry, shouting down at the hordes of children racing about crazily in the courtyard below. The noise is deafening.

"There are about sixty-seven thousand people in this one area alone," McClain says. "So many kids have signed up for the school they have to come in shifts—there are morning classes, and another shift in the afternoon. On this rooftop alone, two hundred and fifty youngsters come for lessons—and for the gospel. This is a wonderful evangelistic opportunity. O.M.S. has three schools in this area, and we're starting more. The tragedy is that there are tens and tens of thousands of other children who can't be helped because we haven't got the money or the personnel. That's why we're trying to stir up people back in the States and make them aware of the need out here."

We go out on one of the balconies and peer into some of the ten-by-twelve cells. The people inside smile as we invade their privacy, but their smiles are timid and hesitant, as though they are not quite certain as to what we want. Most of the rooms are spotlessly clean, but most of the people are in rags and tatters.

"They work if they can find it," McClain says. "But because there are so many, because the city is so congested, there is not much they can do to keep alive. I'll say this, the Hong Kong government has done a magnificent job with these people. It may not seem to you as though much has been done beyond providing them with these cells to live in, but you should have seen Hong Kong before they started putting up these H-blocks."

Down in the courtyard, firecrackers have begun to explode. This is Chinese New Year's Eve, and the noises of the city have been increasing in volume. So has the excitement been increasing—the children's voices are louder and more raucous, and people are rushing every which way, carrying lanterns and trailing long streamers of brightly colored papers.

"In a little while," McClain says, "you won't be able to hear yourself think in Hong Kong."

We go down and get back into the bus, and McClain drives us to the O.M.S. headquarters in Fuk Wing Street. The offices are on the top floor of a nine-story building. We take the elevator up and McClain immediately leads us to the front windows overlooking the street. He pushes them open and gestures toward a building on the other side. "There's the *real* refugee problem in Hong Kong," he says.

On the roof of the building, people have erected twenty-odd shacks, putting them together with whatever materials they have been able to steal or pick up from the streets—bits of fruit crates, pieces of metal from signs, hunks of canvas and cardboard and anything else that conceivably can keep out the elements.

"There are ninety thousand people living on the tops of buildings here," Uncle Bud says. "They have no place else to go. When the owner of the building or the authorities make them get off, they go to another building, sneak upstairs somehow, and stake out their camps. They've got no water, of course, and no sanitary facilities. Everything they have, they must carry up there, and some of those buildings are nine and ten stories high."

"I've been in three mission fields," McClain says, "but I've never seen anything that pulled my heart like this. And this is just one of hundreds and hundreds of buildings scattered all over the colony."

Several people on the rooftop have lighted fires. They move from shack to shack, going about their affairs just as they would if they were living in a village on the ground.

"Some of the people on that roof will die up there," McClain says. "They can't get down, they're so old; they had to be carried up to begin with. Others have fallen sick up there. And others are afraid to leave those poor shacks— they're actually afraid that squatters will come in and take them away from them."

"But what about the government?" I ask.

"There's very little that can be done," McClain says. "The H-block buildings already are overcrowded, and there are more and more people coming in every day. Sometimes it seems that for all it does for these people and the hundreds of thousands like them, Hong Kong is a city without a soul. The mission groups do what they can . . . we take them food, clothing, and give them as much help as we're able to. We try to get the sick ones into hospitals, and we take doctors up there from time to time. But it isn't enough. It's just not enough. You know, they're so pitiful: can you imagine an eighty-year-old woman carrying water up nine flights of stairs? I've seen it many times. Some of them must carry water just to earn money."

"Can't any of them work?" I ask.

"Well, some of the women do. They do embroidery, make gloves, handkerchiefs, and so on. Beautiful work, too—and for wages of six or seven cents a day. The others get by the best they can. Some become thieves, of course. They have to. There is no other way they can get by."

We leave and go down into the street once again. Now the New Year's celebration has begun in earnest. All the buildings are lighted brilliantly and hung with long red streamers marked with golden characters; all over there are balloons and ribbons and lanterns and grotesque masks peering out of windows. The people have cascaded out into the streets: they are walking away their laziness for the New Year, Bob explains. They wander aimlessly, apparently ignoring the firecrackers that explode at their feet and in the air above their heads. They all wear fixed smiles; they all bow when they see faces they know. "The feasts are beginning about now," Bob says. "In many houses, they will go on all night long." The noise seems to increase as he speaks. In Hong Kong, on this night, only the rooftops are silent.

We go to dinner in a restaurant Bob knows. There is not much conversation. Everyone, even those who have seen it before, has been humbled by the sight of the rooftop people. Uncle Bud sits at the table with his hands folded before him, as though at prayer, his fine-featured face fallen into an attitude of sorrow. Presently Dale McClain speaks, and what he says gives me some insight into the workings of the missionary's mind. In his voice, now, is none of the Rotarian hurrah that characterized his conversation in the bus. He is reflective and humble. He says, "For most of the people we've seen, life is nothing but hopelessness. Yet we must try to give them hope—every day, we must try. Every day I thank the Lord for letting me try, and giving me strength. I thank Him for giving me this burden here."

FEBRUARY 8 § HONG KONG

After breakfast we meet with Dale McClain, Uncle Bud Kilbourne, and Dr. Peter Jenkins—a medical missionary working with Immanuel Church, an interdenominational church, and with the Rennie's Mill Church Clinic, which is operated by a Christian organization called the Junk Bay Medical Relief Council. This group also operates a sanitarium called Haven of Hope. World Vision does not support either institution; Dave Morken is hoping that perhaps Bob will find it worthy of support and ask the World Vision board to allocate some money to it. Much of Bob's time on his Far Eastern trips is spent on just such inspections.

Dr. Jenkins is a slender, wiry man, with a good, sensitive face. He had been in China as a missionary until the Reds drove him and his wife out, and he has been working in Hong Kong ever since. On the trip out to Junk Bay he tells me briefly of his conversion. Originally, as a boy in England, he had wanted to be a drafting engineer, but then two events changed his mind. The first was his sister's decision to become a missionary. "I felt that she shouldn't be allowed to carry on all by herself," Dr. Jenkins says. "Then too, I decided that my ambition to be a drafting engineer was a purely selfish one. One Sunday a bloke came and preached at the church I was attending. I don't remember all of what he said, but one expression he used, an illustration, you might say, will stay in my mind as long as I live. He said that if one wanted to follow Christ he had to take up Christ's cross—and the cross was the letter *I*, with the crossbar crossing it out. That was what Christ symbolized—selflessness, the *I* of selfishness crossed out. It made me realize that up to that time my life had been based on what I wanted to do, and be, and that I hadn't taken into consideration that if I wanted to follow him I had to cross out the *I* in my life, too."

While Dr. Jenkins is telling me his story, McClain is steering his bus with the same reckless purpose he had displayed the night before, over a steep mountain road that has no guardrails. That in itself perhaps would not be too bad, but a recent rain has made the roads muddy and slippery. Every few feet the bus lurches perilously close to the edge, and my stomach turns over as I look at the five-hundred-foot drops we are missing. Ahead, McClain is chattering away to Dr. Bob, wrestling with the wheel, and occasionally muttering some such reassuring statement as, "Had a close one here the other day—didn't think I'd make it," or "Look at that view—must be almost a thousand feet down there." Where there is no mud, there are rocks; when we are not sliding toward the precipices, we are bounding toward them.

Beside me, Dr. Jenkins is his usual imperturbable British self. The fact that at any minute the Volkswagen may go over the side, scrambling us together in a tangle of torn and battered bodies, does not appear to occur to him. Nor are Uncle Bud or Bob bothered. As for McClain, he continues to shout above the roar of the motor. We go around another turn, and this time the bus leans farther over than before; for one second it hesitates on the edge of the cliff. Then McClain wrenches the wheel again and we slide inward, back into the eight-inch-deep ruts that pass for road.

It takes us nearly an hour and a half to get up to the site of the sanitarium. There we walk over a winding path, set on a ridge, to the ruins of Rennie's Mill, which are set on a cliff overlooking a group of green frame structures far, far down below in a valley on the edge of the bay. I have to sit down in the doorway of a hut near the ruined mill.

The doctor comes to this spot and goes down to the refugee camp on Monday, Wednesday and Friday of each week; on Tuesday, Thursday and Saturday he goes to the sanitarium which is located at the opposite end of the ridge on which we are standing. This institution was founded by some

deaconesses from the Norwegian Covenant Church. It now
has 130 beds; by the end of the year, Dr. Jenkins hopes to get
it up to 210. The building is set in a beautiful landscape, surrounded by vegetable gardens, overlooking the bay.

"I came out here because they had no medical superintendent," Dr. Jenkins says. "There were only the deaconesses—
and they are nurses, although some of them practice a little
medicine."

Miss Annie Skau, the nurse in charge, comes to meet us.
She is a huge woman with ruddy cheeks; she is more than six
feet tall and at least four feet wide, and it is apparent from
the minute we meet her that her body carries as much kind-
ness as weight. As she tells her story, her eyes shine with the
laughter that is an essential part of her personality.

"From Norway, I came to China in 1938," she says, her native accent heavy but not difficult to understand. "I went to
Shenoi, in Northwest China, to do missionary work in a hospital. I stayed there until the autumn of 1952. Then I got out
. . . and came down here to help with the refugees."

"The Communists took over in 1949," Bob says. "That
means you must have been under them for three years, at
least."

Miss Annie nods her huge head.

"Yes. When they came, we knew it would be difficult.
We asked our Chinese friends what we should do. They
said that if I didn't stay on, it would look as though I wasn't
meant to be a witness for Christ, or a servant. So I stayed."

"Didn't they make it hard for you?"

"Yes, yes, very hard at times. Once when I went for some
meetings in Honan Province, I was arrested and put in jail
for nine days. Another time, for a week. But the wonderful
thing about it was, I was not afraid of them. The Lord gave me

peace in my heart. The first time, the first night in jail, I found the peace . . . I'm not often one to be calling out Hallelujah, but that first night I praised God the whole night through.

"A soldier was guarding outside my cell. He said, 'What are you talking about in there?' I said to him, 'I am praising the Lord, my God.'

"He said, 'He must be a poor God if he puts you in prison.'

"I said, 'No, no, I know He has put me here because He means me to do something, and I am happy.'

"And then the miracle happened. Some Christians in the neighborhood heard that I was in there, and what had happened, and they started the work in defiance of the Communists, and six weeks after that there was a church there. They were arrested time after time, and some of them were tortured, but they kept on and by and by they were left alone by the Communists.

"That was in March, 1950, when they arrested me. The second time was in July of the same year. That time I went down to another part of Honan where we had a mission station. I went down for a week for Bible classes. As I am on my way to go there, a Christian warned me not to go. 'Very dangerous,' this Chinese said. But I wanted to go, and I went. We had good meetings. On the last day, four hundred came. The day after that, I was arrested. Down in that section there had been a Mr. and Mrs. Parker, missionaries of the China Inland Mission. They had a daughter, a Mrs. Mason. The police who arrested me said I was she. They said I was claiming to be Norwegian when I really was an Englishwoman. The church people in that section all went to the Communists and risked their lives, trying to help me. One Chinese woman stood outside my cell, sobbing, begging them to let her come in so that I would not be alone. They all gave me much proof of their love of Christ. Finally the police agreed to release me. They said to the people, "If you are wrong, and we find out that she is the Englishwoman, as we believe she is, your lives all are in danger.'

"I had walked 140 miles to get down there for those meetings, and I then had to walk back to my station. I was weak from the lack of food during the time I had been in the prison, but God gave me strength. It took me five days to get back to my station, but I made it then."

Miss Annie is the only one of the original women who began work in the Rennie's Mill refugee camp. But now her principal interest is the sanitarium. She takes us through and shows us the wards, which are, she says, "Named for the fruits of the spirit—Love, Peace, Patience, Joy."

There are twenty-odd children in the camp, all refugees. "We had one little brother and sister, the girl five and the boy three, who grieved our hearts," Miss Annie says. "They had been forced by the Communists to watch their parents tortured and killed, and then they were turned loose. Some older children took them to some refugees who were coming across the border, and they brought them to the Rennie's Mill camp. Both of them had tuberculosis, and we brought them over here at once. The little girl's face was as stone. It was a long, long time before we could get her to speak, and for months afterward she would awaken in the night and scream because she was dreaming the whole thing all over again."

We have all been listening—and marveling—as this great-bodied, great-hearted woman speaks to us. Bob ventures to ask her where she was born in Norway, and her answer is indicative of her faith.

"I was born in Oslo," she says. "Born there the first time and the second time."

We say good-by to her and go back to our bus. "One of our bigger problems," Peter Jenkins says, "is to get her to take a holiday. She's supposed to have four weeks each year. I believe she's had one week off in the six years she's been out here."

Going up the first mountain on the road back, the Volkswagen is mired down. We all get out and attempt to push as McClain guns the motor in an effort to pull out. After a half-hour's hard work, we finally haul the bus out and get started again.

Back in Kowloon, after lunch, Dave Morken and his wife, Helen, arrive to take us out to see the people who live on the boats in the harbor, and to visit Miss Ethel Groce, who is known as The Boat Lady. Uncle Bud, McClain, and Dr. Jenkins go along, and after a few minutes' drive we reach a wharf where a huge barge is drawn up with several dozen sampans, small scowlike boats none much more than twelve feet long, tied to it with long ropes. Planks reach from the barge to the sampans, which are run by tough-looking, hard-armed Chinese women. I have been in New York Harbor, in London, in Marseilles, and in Yokohama, but I have never seen, nor have I ever been prepared to see, so many small boats gathered together in one section. There must be five thousand of them in the area I can see from where we are standing—boats of every size and shape, sailboats and motor-boats and rowboats and, predominating, the sampans poled along by the stern-faced women.

"Forty thousand people live on these boats," Dr. Jenkins says. "Not all are refugees. Some have been here for many generations. They choose to live this way—they are water people, and they like the life."

"It's actually a boat city," Bob says. "There are theaters on these boats, restaurants, stores, and markets, people who make clothes, cobblers. . . ."

Dr. Jenkins has been dickering with one of the women in the sampans, and now three of them move up to pick up our party. We get into the boats—Reinhold, Bob, and Mrs. Morken in one, Dave and McClain in another, Uncle Bud and Dr. Jenkins and I in a third. The woman with the pole pulls in her rope, dips her pole into the murky, filthy water, and we float out into the harbor.

"What do these people do about schools?" I ask the doctor.

"Well, most of them get no education—unless they turn traitor to their families and go on land," he says. "But the woman I'm taking you to see does have a school she conducts, and there are some other arrangements made for education. But mostly the children grow up in ignorance. And there are many, many children, too, as you can see. Sometimes there are as many as twelve people in a family living on a boat this size."

The boat we are on is less than ten feet long. Over it is a thatched canopy; we are sitting on a strip of worn yellow linoleum. To the rear, in another section, is a small stove and a bucket containing water. Near it are several rolled-up blankets. Our poler obviously lives here—and, for that matter, may have a family. Dr. Jenkins asks her if she does. She rattles off several sentences in Chinese. He turns to me. "She's got nine children," he says.

Wherever we look, people are carrying on every conceivable function aboard the boats. Several of them have chickens in crates lashed to the rear; on one large sampan a goat is tethered. One man is cutting another's hair. An old man with a long beard sits reading a book. A man with a boat laden with bright green cabbages is bargaining with a housewife who is screaming and shaking her head. On one sampan nearby, four men are sitting around a mah-jongg board. Children on single flimsy boards pole themselves up and down from sampan to sampan; another small boy unconcernedly urinates over the side while his mother holds onto one shoulder.

"Theoretically," says Uncle Bud, "you could be born on a boat, grow up, get married, raise children, see them raise children, and die on one of these sampans without ever setting foot on the shore."

As our grim lady gondolier poles us forward, it becomes apparent that the sampans and the other boats are laid out at anchor so that street-channels lie between them. A stranger would lose his way at once; conceivably even someone fairly familiar with the boat city could lose his way if he were not extremely careful. We have been out less than fifteen minutes, and by now the shore is long since lost to sight. All around there is nothing but boats.

As we pass a sampan that is larger than most, I see a man cleaning a fish. "Are most of them fishermen?" I ask the doctor.

"Oh dear no," he says. "The fish that would live in this water hereabouts wouldn't be fit to eat, I daresay—too much excrement in the water, too much slop, too many poisonous organisms. No, some of them are fisherfolk—but to ply their trade, they must go out into the open sea. Most of them work at the same trades that landlocked people do. And, all things considered, quite profitably, too. As I've said, some have been here for many years. They are descendants of people who came down from China in other troubled times. They know nothing but the boat life, and they are quite accustomed to it."

Ahead of us looms a large scow next to a barge, the *Gracious Light*. We go aboard.

§ BOAT LADY

Miss Ethel Groce is a frail lady who speaks in a quiet, almost timorous voice. She looks rather like a schoolmarm, old-fashioned style, which indeed she is, part of the time. The afternoon I visited her, she told me that she never dreamed, when she was a girl, that she would spend most of her adult life aboard a boat in China. Born in Troy, Missouri, she spent a girlhood that was typical of that of any midwestern child from a good family—except, perhaps, for the strong desire she felt to serve God. This was what prompted her to go to school at Moody Bible Institute in Chicago, from which she was graduated in 1931. By then she was determined to be a missionary, but she wanted to go out as a medical missionary, and accordingly enrolled in the nurses' training program at Presbyterian Hospital. She was there three years.

Meanwhile, the course of her life already had been pointed out to her. Missionaries are always so busy doing their chosen work they seldom have time to set down accurate records of their activities. They often behave as though their work always has been—and, in one sense, it has. About all I could learn of the origin of the Oriental Boat Mission, originally called The South China Boat Mission, is that a certain Miss Alexander, an Englishwoman living in Hong Kong, originally was touched by the plight of the people in the harbor. Somehow, she communicated her concern to the young people of the Ewing Street Congregational Church in Chicago. These people raised money to set up a small chapel on the water's edge. The pastor of that church, the Reverend Mr. Edward Drew, became interested in the project. So did his sister Florence. She had taken a special teacher's course at Valparaiso University in 1908, and later had done some mission work in the ghetto in Chicago. Corresponding with Miss Alexander, she heard the call to Hong Kong.

Because she had no money to live on, she had to work first as a secretary in an interdenominational organization. She worked half a day, and spent the other half in the water-edge chapel. A year later, Mr. Drew went out to join her. The trouble was, they felt they were not reaching the boat people properly; the priests of other religions were living on boats right among the harbor dwellers, and the Drews knew that to be effective they too would have to do that. Then they heard that the Swedish Evangelical Free Church of Canton had a boat called *Morning Star*. With the help of some Chicago businessmen, they bought the boat and established headquarters in Canton. Mr. Drew went back to America in 1913 because of illness, but as soon as he recovered he set about raising funds for the project. That was the beginning.

The Drews were followed by other missionaries, who in turn built more boats and floated them all over the South China delta. At one time there were nine. The boats ranged as far upstream as Wu Chow, two hundred miles from Hong Kong.

When Miss Ethel Groce heard her call, she joined the mission and, on a boat named *Proclaiming Light,* went up to Canton.

Most of the Chinese who lived in the small inlets and harbors along the river had never heard the gospel before, and they were intrigued by the woman who stood on the deck of her barge and spoke to them. They went to the services she conducted, and many were converted and went back to their villages to spread the Word. Occasionally they were hostile. More often, they were uncomprehending—but the visions of glory she preached were enough to give them some hope, and most of them welcomed her.

The more Miss Groce saw of the lives of the Chinese, the more determined she was to help them. "The money they might have spent on schools and railroads, they spent on incense and firecrackers," she told me the afternoon I visited her on the *Gracious Light.* "We in the Boat Mission tried to encourage them to start their own schools and to improve their lot." In some villages she invited the women on board to show them sanitary methods of cooking and to let them use her sewing machine.

Little by little, the boat ladies began attracting more followers, and over the years they worked out a regular routine of ports of call. It was a lonely life, for months would often go by in which they did not see another person who spoke English. They seldom heard from their relatives in the States, for they were able to get back to the points where they could receive mail only at rare intervals. Yet they had so much work to do that they did not mind. At one point, one of the boat ladies established a leper colony aboard her craft. It survived there for two years and later moved ashore.

While Chiang Kai-shek and his forces were trying to hold off the Communist rebels, Miss Groce and the rest of the Boat

Mission ladies went quietly about their work. It was not until the latter part of 1947, around Christmas, that they had their first taste of trouble. A few days before the holiday, Miss Groce received an anonymous letter telling her that if she did not move on, the boat and the passengers aboard—the converts who were helping with her work—would be bombed. She was then anchored at Tsing-Yuen.

"We were tempted to pull out, I admit," Miss Groce told me. "And we hesitated. We felt certain that they would not bomb us, American citizens . . . but we knew that if our Chinese were still aboard, they might go ahead and carry out their warning. We told our Chinese to leave us, and we stayed on. We laid it before the Lord, and we felt certain that it was His will that we stay. So we stayed."

In the autumn of 1949, Miss Groce knew she could stay no longer. The Communists were taking over everywhere; all the Christians were fleeing. She floated her boat down to Hong Kong, and she has been in the harbor ever since. Today she is carrying on a program that would tax even a man of more than average strength. First, she holds an inpatient clinic aboard the boat three days each week, treating anywhere from thirty to forty patients for minor ailments (Dr. Peter Jenkins treats those with wounds and diseases which are beyond the scope of Miss Groce's medical skill). Five days each week she conducts a school for eighty children of the boat people. She teaches English in the school; Chinese volunteers, all Christians, teach the other subjects. Grades one, two, and three are taught in the morning; four, five, and six in the afternoon. One boy who attended her classes went on to high school on the mainland, and graduated in June 1959. After her school day is over, she does visitation work among the sampans. On Sunday, with the assistance of a Chinese pastor, she conducts church services in the mornings and evenings. On Wednesday she has a prayer meeting. On other days she conducts a Bible school. She also holds classes in sanitation and other subjects of which the boat people are totally ignorant. In her spare time, she makes minor repairs on her boat.

The *Gracious Light* no longer moves around; it is anchored where the people can find it whenever they want to come to it. Miss Groce goes ashore only once or twice a week, to buy provisions and to pick up her mail. She travels by sampan, usually, and when she hails one of the water taxis she steps carefully from her craft to the other. She has to exercise unusual care. In all the years of living and working on the water, Miss Ethel Groce has never found time to learn to swim.

FEBRUARY 9 § HONG KONG

This morning we go with the Morkens to visit Miss Mildred Dibden, who operates a home for abandoned children and orphans at Fan Ling, a village on the other side of the huge mountain that overlooks Kowloon.

"She has at least ten abandoned babies out there," Mrs. Morken explains, "most of them with some sort of handicaps . . . deformed babies, babies with cleft palates, a spastic. They're practically all girls, because the people don't often abandon boy babies." Mrs. Morken is hoping that World Vision may give Miss Dibden some help.

Miss Dibden's home is in an old police headquarters, a substantial building situated at the top of a steep hill. We are all breathing hard by the time we get to the top. A cluster of four- and five-year-olds is at the door, waiting for us, their bright faces eager and expectant. When we start toward the door, they all vanish into the dark building. We can hear them giggling and whispering in the shadows. We go inside. To the left is a room, roughly twenty by twenty feet, in which eight or nine tiny girls, none much older than two, are solemnly sitting on chamber pots. They look at us, all of them, with that expression of delight-in-accomplishment and knowledge-of-pleasing-the-adult that occurs on a child's face only when it is being successfully toilet-trained. We all turn away from the door to keep from laughing aloud, and then Miss Dibden, a commanding figure in a blue uniform, comes down to welcome us. She shows us through her home, indicating the classrooms, the sleeping rooms, and the small infirmary. She has no trained help here; only a local girl or two, to help her with the children.

Miss Dibden is British, which is about the only personal information I can extract from her. Each time I attempt to ask her about herself, she looks alarmed and exclaims, "Oh, I wouldn't want my name mentioned. . . . Oh, I daresay we shouldn't put anything in about *me*." After approximately a half-hour of interrogation, I come up with the following facts:

Miss Dibden came to Hong Kong as a young girl.

She came out under the auspices of a missionary society— she will not say which one—as a teacher.

She spent three and a half years in a foundling home, but she will not say which one.

She returned to England, but she will not say to which city, town or village.

While working in the nameless home she learned of the children who are abandoned in Hong Kong every day and resolved that she had to help them.

Upon returning to England she went to the nameless missionary society and said she had heard a call to set up a home for abandoned children, but the nameless director had said that she was not trained for such work, and that in any case the nameless missionary society was not equipped to support such work, and that if she would only wait five years the society might consider it.

Now, as she swings into the story of her work, Miss Dibden becomes more informative and factual.

"In those days, only the Roman Catholics were doing anything for abandoned babies," she says. "I did not see that I was too young to do that work. I thought I was old enough, and I said to the missionary director—"

"What did you say his name was?" I ask, trying to catch her up.

"I did not say," says Miss Dibden, her gray-topped, sunburned face becoming rather severe. Suddenly I realize the reason behind her reticence. She does not want to blame a servant of the Lord for his refusal to assist in another part of the Lord's work. From here on the interview becomes easier.

"I said to him, 'I must go back. God wants me to do this work, and I must find a way to do what is God's will.' As I say, only the Catholics were doing the job. They had two homes for abandoned children. And they had many more than they could cope with. Babies were dying like flies in the streets.

"To train myself as a nurse, I went to Bristol Southmead Hospital and began working in the dispensary. Every day I learned more, and after ten months I had all I needed to know, I thought. Then I began applying to various missionary societies, asking to be sent out, but they all turned me down.

"Presently, on a train trip to Red Hill, in Surrey, I met a woman I had known in Hong Kong, Mrs. Lechmere Clift. She was the wife of the man who had started the Immanuel Medical Mission in Hong Kong. I told her all about my plan, and how I could not find anyone to help. She asked me to come back to Hong Kong. 'At least think about it,' she said. I thought about it and prayed and it seemed to be the open door I was seeking. In due course I wrote her and said I would be coming out. Another month passed. They meanwhile had taken in the first abandoned child before I got there. It was six weeks old. Mrs. Clift's houseboy took care of it in his room."

Miss Dibden arrived in Hong Kong on November 9, 1926. She went straight to the mission and collected the baby and moved into a room. Then she went looking for furniture. The baby's first bed was a drawer in a chest. The other drawers soon were filled, and before long, with the help of the Clifts, she was able to take a small house. That was in Hong Kong proper. When World War II broke out, she had ninety-eight babies under her care; the oldest was four and a half. She took the lot and went out to Fan Ling on the day the Japanese came into the Crown Colony. She found a house there to live in, but the house was all she had.

"We had no milk and no food for the babies," she says. "That is, no proper food. For the first three months, it was horrible. We had some rice and some water from boiling greens, and that was all there was to eat. Their little limbs shrank to nothing, their stomachs were bloated and distended, and we saw them dying before our eyes and there was nothing we could do but pray. All the tiny ones died. We lost sixty children in the first six months, and much of the time we were too weak even to bury them properly. We would shovel away a few inches of dirt and cover them up. They kept dying, some from malnutrition and some from exposure . . . it was a very cold winter, and we did not have proper clothing or coverlets for them. There was nothing, nothing we could do but sit and watch them die.

"Then, unexpectedly, some help came from the enemy. There was a Japanese camp near our camp. The commanding officer, Colonel Kaumaui, had a sister back in Japan who was a Christian. He gave us some condensed milk and a few other supplies, and he and his men began sending in children they had found. They tried to help us in whatever way they could, but they themselves had so little, there was not much they could do."

After a time, the Colonel was moved out of that area. Miss Dibden and her brood had supplies for only a few days, and then she knew she would have to get help elsewhere. She decided to appeal to the Japanese in the city. It is approximately twenty-one miles from Fan Ling to Hong Kong. She walked all the way, taking a few of the stronger children with her, and confronted the commander of the first Japanese installation she came to.

"What are you going to do about these children?" she demanded.

The officer said there was nothing he could do. The children were not his responsibility. Miss Dibden walked on and on, and was rebuffed time and again. Presently she came to a sympathetic man who agreed to help her. Once each month, for the three and a half years that the Japanese held the Crown Colony, Miss Dibden went to beg for her babies. After the first few journeys her shoes came apart, and from then on she walked the distance in her bare feet.

By the time the British reoccupied Hong Kong, the population of her little home had swelled again to 102. The Japanese had kept dumping babies on her doorstep, and she had gone on caring for them.

In 1951 she went back to England for a time, but the call of the place she had established was too strong, and she returned to Hong Kong and set up shop again. Today the home is partially supported by the Christian Children's Fund. Helen Morken does what she can to assist in providing support.

Miss Dibden's troubles are not over. "Even this day I am in trouble with the authorities," she says. "They want to take my older girls away from me and send them to vocational schools."

This explains Miss Dibden's reluctance to say anything that might get her into further trouble. Government officials in every land have a way of grasping at one technical point and using it to keep the frequently senseless machinery of government moving. It might be that they could say that she is inadequately trained, that she lacks official blessing, or that by accepting children who are brought to her she is not going through the required red tape. She is terrified of what they might do to her. She has always thought of the home as the living place of a family, and of herself as the children's mother. "Why, already one girl has brought me a 'grandchild,'" she says happily. "And there will be others. Many of my girls have married; nearly all of them—the early ones—are working. And all are Christians. All have accepted Christ as their Savior. That is why I want to go on with my work."

We leave Miss Dibden and go back to our hotel. It is nearly time to catch the aircraft for Bangkok, and we say good-by to

Dave and Helen, McClain, Uncle Bud, and Dr. Jenkins. On
the way to the airport, I try to sort out my impressions of the
day. Next to the sight of those hopeless people living in the
icehouse in Taegu, I believe that those rooftop dwellers affected me more than anything I have seen on this trip. I cannot
get them out of my head. The memory of their plight, and
the accompanying echoes of the things Dave, McClain, and
the doctor told me, affect me so that I began comparing the
lives of those three and the rest of my new friends with the life
I lead. Mine seems empty and pointless when I compare it
with theirs, and this realization is disquieting, even unnerving.
Before I quite know the course of my thoughts, I am thinking
of what I do for a living in the States, of the stories I write
about the film stars and the Broadway actors, the chronicles
of crime and violence, the articles about good things to eat
and new ways to prepare them. For my wife and me, it has
never been a question of when we eat, or *will* we eat? It has
been the pleasurable contemplation of what we will eat next,
or of where we will eat. And the same always has been true of
most of my friends. I personally know no one who ever
starved. No relative of mine ever had leprosy, none had to
hide from head-hunters, and none ever saw their homes
washed away by floods or shaken to the ground by earth-
quakes. I think of the incredible poverty of the people whom
these missionaries are serving, of the children gathered in
from the streets, of the lepers who sit in darkness waiting to
die, of the old women pulling themselves up the dark flights
of stairs to carry a tomato can of contaminated water to earn
a fraction of a cent—and as these things come to me I reflect
that Dale McClain, in a single ten-minute visit to a family living on a rooftop, does more than I do for my fellow man in a
year. I amuse; he serves. What I feel is not a sense of guilt,

precisely; it is a sense of inadequacy and of pointlessness. I think of Howard Moffett, getting up from his dinner to go out into the noisy Korean market to price long underwear. I think of Bjarne Gislefoss saving part of his ridiculous monthly salary to buy a refrigerator in which to keep plasma. I think of Lil Dickson walking into the hills with her rat-chewed bag. I think of Irene Webster-Smith and the Kaji sisters. I think of the others—the hesitant Mildred Dibden, the reticent Miss Groce, and I begin to feel strongly that I, too, ought to be serving in some way similar to theirs, and as this feeling goes through me I realize that I am hoping that I can, and that my hope is so powerful it is more than a hope, it is almost a prayer.

I glance at Bob, sitting next to me in this taxi that is taking us to the airport. "You look beat, Bob," I say.

"I am tired," he says. "I can't deny it. You can't go on listening to everybody's burden, and seeing everybody's burden, all day long, day after day, and not get tired . . . not if you care. And we all care. But you've got to forget that you're tired and remember that there are millions here who are more tired than you are, and doubly so because they know no Savior, and are not rested and comforted by the Word of God."

It occurs to me that I really do not know this man well, and I begin asking him questions about himself. On the flight from Hong Kong to Bangkok, he tells me some of his story. . . .

§ JET-PROPELLED PREACHER

A battered brown leather suitcase, always packed and ready, stands in the vestibule just inside the door of Dr. Bob Pierce's house in Arcadia, California. It bears no airline tags or stickers from exotic hotels, but during the past ten years this suitcase, which contains a kit of toilet articles, a couple of changes of khaki work shirts and pants, a plain business suit, and some socks and underwear, has traveled around the world more than a dozen times. To Pierce's wife, Lorraine, and to his three daughters, it is a symbol of the husband and father they seldom see, because he is seldom home. To Pierce himself, it is a symbol of the work he feels God put him on earth to do—work that continually carries him to remote lands where hundreds of thousands of people need help, and, more important, hope.

Inside the suitcase is a Bible, stained and spotted and falling apart. On its flyleaf is written:

"Let my heart be broken with the things that break the heart of God."

This is Bob Pierce's prayer and creed. A robust, dynamic man of forty-five, Pierce is humble and self-effacing. He has never sought publicity for himself and his work in the United States. This book will be something of an embarrassment to him. He is all but unknown in his own country. But leaders of many Asiatic countries regard him as one of America's most important unofficial ambassadors.

Bob Pierce is an ordained Baptist minister, but World Vision, the organization of which he is the founder and president, is interdenominational. Its aim is to give assistance to those who need it, whoever they may be, wherever they may be, whatever their emergency, spiritual or physical. It has five primary objectives—to stimulate public interest in missionary work, to conduct evangelistic campaigns, to hold conferences of native pastors and key Christian leaders, to promote and expand social-welfare services, and to give emergency aid to churches, missions, hospitals, and other institutions.

Since 1950, when World Vision was founded, Bob has traveled more than 2,500,000 miles to administer this ambitious program. He cannot stop traveling. As quickly as he gets one project in one country running smoothly, another one claims his attention. "Somehow," says his wife, "he seems to sense where he is needed." Bob denies this ability. "God sends me," he says, with characteristic simplicity.

In the winter of 1956, when the Hungarian patriots were attempting to revolt against their Communist rulers, Bob was returning home from an exhausting three months of work in the Far East. Traveling on his missions, he drives himself mercilessly, rising at dawn and working through to midnight; often the only sleep he gets consists of naps he snatches en route from one spot to another. This time he was bone-weary. He planned to stop in London to address a Christian conference, stay overnight in New York to meet with some supporters of World Vision, and then go on to the West Coast for a week of rest with his wife and daughters. When his plane stopped in Istanbul, he heard that the Hungarian revolt was being crushed and that thousands of refugees were streaming into Austria. He knew that World Vision's funds were low; he had pledged nearly all its money in Asia. But he has supreme confidence: "I believe with all my heart that if God gives you a task to do He will provide the means to do it," he says, "because I've seen it happen time and again." He wired his headquarters for a large sum, interrupted his trip home, and spent the next three weeks on the Hungarian border ministering to the fleeing patriots—distributing blankets, clothing, and medical supplies.

That instance was so characteristic as to be commonplace in the life of Bob Pierce, but it does not begin to tell even a part of the story of World Vision. During the Korean War he became accredited as a correspondent for a magazine, but spent most of his time doing evangelistic and relief work among Allied and Korean troops. He traveled up and down the lines continuously, conducting services for the fighting men and going into compounds to visit prisoners. It struck him that something would have to be done about the orphans after the war. The armed forces and the UN agencies already were doing what they could, up to the limit of their funds, but children were being orphaned in such numbers that drastic measures had to be taken. "Everywhere I went, I saw children wandering the streets, living like animals," Pierce recalls. "I saw babies who had nothing to drink but contaminated water." The Christian Church in Korea was demoralized. Hundreds of church buildings had been burned and the congregations scattered. More than five hundred Korean pastors, among them many of Pierce's friends, had been killed; others had gone into hiding.

Pierce was carrying a motion-picture camera. He took many rolls of film. When he returned to the United States, he began showing the films and also speaking to raise money to send back to the orphans. He had no specific program of fund distribution—he sent some to a Baptist missionary in one area, some to a Presbyterian in another, other sums to members of any denomination in dire need. When he went back to Korea a few months later and found that this haphazard assistance was not enough, he went right to work raising more money to build new orphanages and to add facilities to those already in existence. These buildings were turned over to their operators at once. This always has been Pierce's policy: once he undertakes and finishes a construction project, he deeds it to the Christian agency that will use it, and then usually goes on supplying funds for its upkeep.

By early 1959, the program that had started in the Korean trenches was supporting more than 13,000 children in 152 havens in the Far East. On November 3, 1958, Chang Whan Sohn, Minister of Health and Social Affairs in Korea, wrote Pierce, "No one can doubt that your untiring efforts have entitled you to be called Father of the Korean Orphans." On May 8, 1959, President Syngman Rhee awarded Pierce the Republic of Korea's Medal for Public Welfare Service. In a service held in Kyung Mu Dai, the Korean White House, the eighty-four-year-old President said:

"Dr. Pierce has endeared himself to the people of Korea. His high ideals for mankind and untiring ministrations guided by his religious principles are deeply appreciated. . . ."

When Pierce first began aiding the orphans, he simply collected money and sent it on. Today, he makes it possible for citizens in the States to "adopt" orphans by contributing ten dollars per month for each child. Some contributors have taken on more than one orphan. Roy Rogers, the cowboy star, and his wife, Dale Evans, have supported eighteen. Because he uses the word "adopt," Pierce continually receives requests from people who wish to bring children to the

United States to live. But he emphasizes that he is not operating an adoption agency, although on occasion he has shepherded children to this country after they have been legally adopted through accredited agencies.

Once, while bringing back nineteen Korean-American children, the issue of Korean girls and American soldiers, Pierce stopped overnight in Japan. An assistant reported that there seemed to be something wrong with one of the little girls. Pierce brought in a doctor, who immediately diagnosed the child's trouble as measles. At once the other eighteen children also came down with it. Pierce and his band were quarantined for two weeks.

Most of the orphanages in Korea are staffed by native workers, which frees the missionaries from the States to do other work. That is, to do the work they can afford to do. Nearly all missionaries function on extremely limited budgets. Many earn salaries of less than fifty dollars a month, and many of them actually contribute much of their own money to the projects dearest to their hearts. A part of Pierce's program which is even more important to him today than the orphanage work (which is now running smoothly) is raising emergency funds for missionaries who want to undertake new projects or to expand those already existing. When he hears of a missionary, a pastor, a mission, or a hospital in dire need, he investigates personally. If he is satisfied that the need is real, he reports to the World Vision board of directors. The members of the board, all of whom serve without salary, have long since ceased to be surprised at the diversity of the projects.

"Wherever there's somebody working for the Lord who needs emergency assistance, we try to provide it," Pierce says. "This makes our work very broad. We never know what we'll find. For example, we send funds to help a Christian radio station in the south of Korea that's beaming programs toward the Communist area in the north. We subsidize the purchasing agency of the Evangelical Foreign Mission Association in New York. Missionaries who need any worthwhile thing can write to that organization and get it practically at cost: an operating table, a tape recorder, bandages, bedding, or food supplies.

"Then too, we have many specific small projects. We're helping a man who is surveying all of the portions of the world where Christ has never been preached. The information he gathers will eventually be made available to all denominations.

"Two missionaries from Saskatchewan are working in the bush country in the southwestern part of Ethiopia, two are in Quito, Ecuador; we help them. We sent a car to a missionary in South Africa. We pay the salary of a secretary to a missionary in Calcutta. We bought the beds for a sanitarium in Tokyo. We heard of a young man in Punjab who wanted to become a pharmacist. We investigated, and found he planned to go back and help his neighbors. We decided to send him to school. . . ."

Today, World Vision sponsors more than 250 such projects, in twenty-five countries. Since 1950, it has disbursed over $5,000,000. Pierce raises this money by preaching both in person and on the radio, and by sending out mail appeals.

In early 1958, a man who had spent more than forty years in the Far East as a missionary turned up at the World Vision headquarters in Pasadena, California. He told his story to Pierce. He was seventy; his church had retired him and sent him back to the United States. His wife was dead; he had no relatives. He had a small pension to live on, but he had no place to go. "I speak Chinese, and I know I could still be useful in Asia," he told Pierce, "but no one will send me out." Pierce immediately telephoned his widely scattered board members, and within a week the old missionary was bound for Hong Kong. Pierce had found an organization that needed his services. World Vision paid for his transportation.

It is difficult to pry such stories out of Pierce. Disdaining any personal involvement, he declares that he is only the instrument of God's work. One of the guiding principles of his life, he says, is a paraphrase from a Dutch translation of an Old Testament verse: "All that we have comes from God, and we give it out of His hand." He says he never feels that he himself owns anything; that everything he has is given to him to pass on to others. This lack of concern for material things sometimes worries his board members (Claude Edwards, president of a supermarket chain; Dr. Richard C. Halverson, minister of the Fourth Presbyterian Church, Washington, D.C.; Dr. F. Carlton Booth, professor of Evangelism, Fuller Seminary, Pasadena; and Cliff Barrows, a permanent member of the Billy Graham Team). "Bob thinks of money only as something with which he can help others," one World Vision official said recently. "He's always overcommitting the organization. We'll say to him, 'Bob, go easy,' and he'll say, 'All right,' and the next day he'll talk us into building a hospital."

Pierce was openhanded even in the days when he had nothing to give away. Years ago, he says, it was demonstrated to him that any act of assistance is returned a hundredfold, in the manner of the bread cast upon the water. He had just begun his preaching career and was working in a Los Angeles rescue mission. A derelict asked him for some money. "I may look like a drunk," the man said, "and the truth is, I was. I used to be an instructor in an upstate college but the tensions of the work, plus certain emotional problems, caused me to begin drinking. Before long I lost everything—my position, my home, and finally, because I couldn't stop, my wife and three children. I've been wandering around trying to keep myself from going completely to pieces. If you could stake me to some food—"

Pierce had two dollars in his pocket. His wife and children were staying with friends who believed in the rescue work he was then doing. He knew well enough that most bums made up such stories only to get money for drink. Yet he unhesitatingly gave the money, keeping only carfare to get home. The man told him he was staying in a flophouse and gave him the address. Next day, Pierce went around to see him, taking food. He prayed with the man and felt that he was helping him. But on his next visit, the man had disappeared. Pierce felt a profound disappointment. He was not so disillusioned that he ceased to make sacrifices on the spur of the moment—he continued to do that—but every time he thought of the man, he felt sad. "I thought maybe I hadn't done enough for him. Maybe I didn't pray enough."

Twelve years later, after he preached a sermon in Moody Church, Chicago, Pierce was approached by a man who looked vaguely familiar. It was the derelict—well-dressed, obviously prosperous, completely rehabilitated. Pierce had started him on the road to recovery, he said. After their prayer, he had decided that he would begin at once to seek God's help for his life. He had taken a job, had saved a little money, had moved on to another job, and eventually had become an executive in a transportation company. "Your prayers helped me to help myself," he told Pierce. Today the man is a faithful contributor to World Vision.

Pierce's pleas for funds are not directed at the rich. Most of the money for the global program trickles in a dollar or two at a time. He prefers it that way: "I would rather have eighty thousand people praying for us and giving us a dollar apiece, than one man giving us eighty thousand dollars. It isn't just the money—it's the power of those prayers. I've seen them work when dollars could do nothing." Also, he feels he does not have time to go out and "sell" potential big contributors. "I live my life in too much of a rush," he says. This is true. He is late for appointments more often than not, and he once took off on a flight for Japan on thirty minutes' notice. Airline traffic managers in Tokyo, Taipeh, Calcutta, and New Delhi have more than once held planes because they knew Pierce was on the passenger list. Yet, curiously, he never appears to be rushed. After streaking across a landing strip, coat flying, suitcase swinging, to catch a plane the motors of which are already warming up, he will find a seat, fasten the belt, and calmly take out his old Bible and begin to read. His demeanor is that of a man at peace with himself and his God.

A friend who accompanied Pierce on a trip to Seoul, Korea, to conduct a conference of native pastors in the autumn of 1957 recalls another example of Pierce's pervading faith. "It had begun to rain several days before the conference was to be held," this man says, "and everybody was frantic with worry. Many of those ministers had traveled four or five hundred miles to attend that conference. Some even had sneaked across the border from Communist North Korea— if they had been caught, it would have meant certain death.

"Yet the rain did not stop. While everybody else on the team was going crazy, Bob went quietly about his preparations, receiving the ministers, reading his Bible, preparing his sermon. At 4 A.M.—the man never seems to sleep—he called me in. 'Pray,' he said. 'Let's all of us pray. And send telegrams to the friends back home, asking them to pray that it stops. We must not disappoint these people. If we ask God for help, He will not disappoint these people.' "

The friend's voice is full of wonder as he continues this story. "I sent the wires. We all prayed. And twenty minutes before the meeting was to begin, it stopped raining and the sun came out. It was a magnificent day.

"You know, I don't believe it just *stopped*. I honestly believe God heard our prayers. And Bob never doubted for a minute that He would."

Robert Willard Pierce was born in Fort Dodge, Iowa, October 8, 1915, the son of Fred A. Pierce, a carpenter who was also a lay minister in first the Methodist church and later in the Church of the Nazarene. Bob began going to Sunday school as soon as he was able to walk. He joined the Church of the Nazarene at eleven, in Southern California, where his father had taken the family to live.

The Pierces were never well off. Bob took on a variety of jobs in order to help out at home, but his extracurricular activities did not prevent him from becoming an honor student both at Washington High School in Los Angeles and at Pasadena College, where, in his junior year, he was elected president of the student body. In college he met and fell in love with Ruth Lorraine Johnson, whom he married in 1936. Lorraine was the daughter of a minister, and it was partly because of conversations with his father-in-law, Pierce says, that the call to evangelism became so strong that he felt that he had to leave college and become actively involved in the Lord's work.

For eighteen months, he and his bride traveled up and down the West Coast while Bob preached in one small church after another. Members of the congregations put him up overnight, fed him, and sent him on to other parishes. Often he and Lorraine hitchhiked. He lived only on what the congregations could afford to pay him. For the first time in his life, he was truly happy. He began taking courses at night, in theology and public speaking, making up the work he had missed by leaving school. Pierce today is a masterful, compelling speaker —not only because of his encyclopedic knowledge of the Bible, but because his deep, devout faith is evident in every sentence he utters. In Asia, he has to speak principally through interpreters (he knows some Chinese, a little Japanese, and a smattering of other languages), but the conviction and burning intensity always carry through to his listeners.

In 1942 Bob was ordained a minister in the First Baptist Church of Wilmington, California, but by then, after his experiences as an itinerant preacher, could not help feeling that he could do more as an evangelist than as a parish leader. He joined the Los Angeles Evangelistic Center and again began traveling. World War II did not interrupt his career. After trying to enlist as a chaplain and being turned down because of poor vision, he took up the craft he had learned from his father—carpentry—and went to work in a shipyard near Los Angeles. "He would come home from work dead tired," Lorraine Pierce recalls, "but that did not stop him from going out at night to preach wherever he was needed."

Pierce says that 1944 was the turning point in his life. He had met Dr. Torrey M. Johnson, an evangelist who, with Billy Graham, was forming an organization called Youth For Christ International. They asked him to join them, and he accepted. The movement gained tremendous support almost from its inception. Pierce was assigned to be director of the Seattle, Washington, branch. He spent more than a year there, then went on the road, traveling back and forth across the country much as the old-time evangelists had done. Everywhere he went, he drew capacity audiences. Characteristically, he declares that the large crowds were not there just to hear him. "I had the Eureka Jubilee Singers with me," he says. "I know the people came to hear and see them, rather than to listen to me. But when the singers were finished, I had the audience. They had to listen." During the next few years he spoke in churches, tents, civic auditoriums, and in the streets in nearly every major city in the United States. "There was much satisfaction in the thousands we saw converted," he says, "but still there was something lacking. I didn't know what it was. I couldn't define it. I prayed God to point it out to me. And he did."

It happened in 1947, when he was invited by a group of missionaries to spend the summer in China. He flew out and at once fell in love with the land. Between July and October he traveled about holding meetings, a minimum of two a day, sometimes as many as seven. "I kept account of the people who came forward and professed their conversion to Christ," he told me, "on the flyleaf of my Bible—the one I still carry in my suitcase." At the end of the trip he found that he had seen 17,000 people make some definite step toward Christ. He realized that he had found his calling at last—but at the same time, he realized he had not done enough. "I saw indescribable poverty and privation out there," he says, "and hundreds of thousands of people existing in religions that held out no hope for their salvation. They had nothing; they hoped for nothing. Then I saw those same conditions become endurable for people who embraced Christianity—and for others, because those who experienced Christ suffered, but not for nothing. They died, but not without hope."

It seemed to Bob Pierce that God had shown him his burden. From then on his energy had a new purpose. As soon as he returned to the United States he began traveling and showing the films he had taken. In nine months he raised $65,000 for the Youth For Christ International movement. He returned to China in August 1948. The country then was torn by civil war, and to Bob's horror he learned that many of the Chinese pastors he had met on his previous trip had been murdered or imprisoned by Communists. Missions, schools, and hospitals had been sacked and burned. Christians had been killed by the hundreds. Many missionaries were under house arrest.

In 1949 Bob Pierce decided that an organization of broader aims was necessary to carry on the work he felt Christ had asked him to do. In Portland Oregon, he found a youth leader of like mind, Dr. Frank Phillips, and the two of them planned a campaign to help missionaries meet their emergency needs. This was the beginning of World Vision, Inc. Dr. Phillips was to be the man in charge of organization and details; Pierce was to be the field scout and evangelist. They had no money to start with, which did not disturb them in the slightest. Each began to travel again throughout the country to raise funds with which to send Pierce back. Once back, he found more projects for which funds were needed. It became an endless chain—and since then, his life has followed a pattern to which few men could fit themselves gracefully. He goes to the Orient to aid and survey, makes films, returns to the United States, raises money, sends it back, goes back again, finds new projects, and so on ad infinitum.

Pierce's schedule during 1959 was typical. After the extensive trip which this book chronicles, he returned to the United States to fill a series of speaking engagements. He then went to Osaka, Japan, for the evangelistic crusade described at the end of this book. After going to Australia to address an Anglican Missionary Conference, he returned to Japan to follow up the Osaka Crusade, went back to the United States for more lectures, embarked upon the first half of his pastors' conference schedule, returned to the States again, then went back and completed his conferences.

His energy is often too much for his associates. One says, "The normal man can't keep up with Bob." They fear for his health—which is unnecessary, since he has a lumberman's appetite and the capacity for feeling refreshed after a few hours' sleep. Still, all his friends are continually urging him to slow down. Bob appreciates their solicitude, but it sometimes irritates him. In Osaka, during his evangelistic crusade, one friend begged him to get some rest. He had been sleeping an average of three hours per night, preaching three or four times each day, and between sessions meeting with people who had made decisions for Christ during his sermons. "Get rest?" he demanded. "Slow down? How can anybody slow down when half of Asia goes to bed hungry and without knowing Christ?"

FEBRUARY 10 § BANGKOK

Thailand is a small country populated by small people, and since we have been here only overnight, so that Bob can meet with a minister who is helping in a project scheduled for the summer, the sum of our impressions is small. On our way in from the airport yesterday we passed monks dressed in orange robes walking to temples we saw in the distance. The monks and the ornate temples and the houses on stilts at the sides of the road, the exotic trees and the green fields all were thrown into sharp relief by the shimmering sunlight. In Formosa and Hong Kong, there was a continual haze over the lands, and the sunlight seemed to be filtered; here, the colors are brighter. Yesterday evening, after we checked into our hotel, a surprisingly modern establishment for this aged city, we wandered out into the streets to poke about in the shops, looking at the brass tableware for which Siam is famous, the inlaid-enameled jewelry, and the Buddha heads allegedly picked up in ruins but more probably (Bob says jokingly) made in a small ruin factory somewhere outside town. After dinner, Bob said he had something to show me. "We've seen human degradation on this trip," he said, "but we haven't seen anything like this. This is an area we have not yet been able to do anything about . . . but we're prayin' that someday we'll be able to do something to help." And he took me to an opium den.

The place was located in the Chinese section, which, Bob said, reminded him more of the real China than even the native quarters of Hong Kong. Chinese make up about a third of Thailand's population, and they control most of the country's trade. Darkness was falling when we reached the street where the den was located, but there were hundreds of tiny shops throwing out light, and scores of fires from the carts of the sidewalk food vendors. These vendors were everywhere, each with a cart containing a cookstove, a bowl, a pile of bamboo shoots and vegetables and small bits of meat; the people stepped up, made a sign, and the vendor threw ingredients into the bowl, sloshed in some rice wine, threw some soy sauce after it, let the mixture simmer for thirty seconds, then dumped it all into a copy of the *Bangkok Times* and handed it over to the customer. The food smelled delicious; the aromas followed us through the festive streets. Inside the door of the opium den a man sat on a platform, naked except for a pair of shorts, diligently scraping out the bowls of pipes. "He's salvaging opium that might be left in the bowl," Bob said. The man did not look at us; he went on about his work, frowning as he scraped away. "Opium is now a government monopoly," Bob said. "This is a government-licensed den." I stared at him, certain he was joking. "I'm serious," he said. "Opium is one of the big industries of this country. It's shipped from here all over the world." We go into the den itself, a huge, dimly lighted room filled with three-decked bunks. On each bunk was an addict; on some there were two or three. Some were asleep with beatific or pained expressions; others were staring straight ahead, far from awareness of anything going on about them. All were so thin, so shrunken and wasted it did not seem possible that they could live much longer. The stench in the air was cloyingly sweetish

and heavy, that of the opium combined with the stench of
the filthy bodies and the mustiness of the den itself. As we
passed one bunk, the occupant looked up and smiled; his teeth
were dark brown and green, and his skin had no flesh between it and his bones. He beckoned to us like a man in a semi-
coma, and held up his pipe for us to try. I backed away hastily
and into another aisle. There, prone, were more men who
had been carried to the bunks by attendants to sleep off the
drug's effect, so that the smoking-bunks could be left free for
new customers. "They'll sleep like that until tomorrow,"
Bob said, "and then they'll go out and get some job to earn a
few cents so they can come back here and smoke again.
They've deserted their wives, their children, their homes, their
regular jobs—if they ever *had* any regular jobs. They've deserted everything but the opium and the false world it makes
for them. . . ." The second floor was exactly like the first,
except that the men seemed more settled, so to speak. A few
of them had brightly colored pictures, cut from Siamese
magazines, tacked to the walls. Some had bundles of rags in
the bunks with them: spare clothing, used for pillows.

Later I asked Bob what, if anything, the churches were trying to do for the addicts.

"Not much, I'm afraid," he said. "Siam has never been receptive to the Christian message. The people are strongly
Buddhist—most Thai men spend a few years in the priest-
hood as a matter of course. The Roman Catholics came out
in the sixteenth century, and the Protestants got here in
the nineteenth. There was one man from the Netherlands
Missionary Society, Dr. Karl Gutzlaff, who translated most
of the Bible into Thai and parts of it into Lao and Cambodian,
but in the time he spent in the country he baptized only one
convert, a Chinese. As a matter of fact, most of the converts to

Christianity have been Chinese. A Baptist missionary named William Dean came to Bangkok early in the 1830s, hoping he could get to China through Siam. He organized the first church among the Chinese around 1861. In 1914 the Baptists gave up and went home, but they left a fairly strong Chinese church behind them. The Presbyterians founded hospitals, schools, and churches around the same time, but until recently the work hasn't grown much. The Christian and Missionary Alliance worked twelve years and could reach only about eighty converts, but since World War II they have been expanding their activities, and they're now in nineteen provinces in the eastern part of the country. They're training national pastors and evangelists. The Anglican Church is here, with some schools and a hospital. The Seventh-day Adventists do a good deal of medical work and distribute literature. Since China was closed, members of the China Inland Mission Overseas Missionary Fellowship have come in."

"What is World Vision doing here?"

"We're holding a pastors' conference here in the summer," he said. "I'll tell you more about the Conferences later on. . . ."

Now it is morning, and time for us to leave Bangkok. At the airport, we meet the Reverend Mr. Taeyong, a slight, smiling man with wispy white hair, who has come to discuss the conference. It is planned for July. "We will have only about sixty ordained men," Pastor Taeyong explains, "and there will be some who won't understand English. *Or* Thai. But we will have translators."

"Can't we get the ministers who aren't ordained, too?" Bob asks. "They ought to be with us."

"Oh, yes," the preacher says. "And the evangelists, too. All told we should have over two hundred people. And to address them, two Asiatics and your team of three Americans. The Thai government will give the pastors who must make the journey a special rate on the railroads . . . we've arranged that. One of the schools in Bangkok will change its schedule so that we will have classrooms and dormitories. . . ."

Bob's eyes are twinkling. "You must specify," he says, "that no fare will be paid unless the pastors attend *all* the meetings. We're not just giving them a free trip to Bangkok."

"Oh, yes. *All* the meetings."

"Well," Bob says, "the Lord is blessing us here. I'm proud of you, Brother Taeyong. It looks as though you've got everything ready."

"With God's help," the pastor says.

After the Reverend Mr. Taeyong has left us, Bob says, "That man has done a wonderful job of organization. We'll have ministers there who come from the deepest jungles. Some of them have never even seen shoes, let alone worn them. Some of them will come down the river a hundred fifty, two hundred miles, just to get acquainted with fellow Christians, share experience, and learn more about the Bible.

"Now I want to tell you a little about what our pastors' conferences can mean to these people—I'll tell you in particular about a fellow named Ba Aye. . ."

§ A PASTOR NAMED BA AYE—
AND 20,000 OTHERS

Ba Aye, Bob told me, is the pastor of Elephant Mountain, which is located in the Southern Shan States of Burma. He ministers to the people of his own small village and those who live in other buildings in the area, members of a tribe called the Taungthu. Larry Ward, editor of the *World Vision Magazine*, visited him in the summer of 1959. He described the trip later as follows:

"Getting to see Ba Aye wasn't easy. First we flew several hundred miles north from bustling Rangoon, watching as the flat semijungle country below changed to rolling hills and then to rugged mountains. Then we climbed via jeep for some twenty miles of winding but fairly comfortable road, marveling as we went at the panorama of green valleys spreading far out below us and the breath-taking vista of still higher mountains ahead. Then we left the paved highway to bounce along a deeply rutted road . . . and when even that road ended, we still kept going. I shook my head in amazement time and again as the sturdy jeep plowed its way on up the mountainside through fields of big boulders, even crashing when necessary through the scrubby bush and small trees. But finally the jeep could go no farther. The sky had clouded, and it had begun to rain in great, driving sheets—and the ground beneath us had turned into an oozy, slippery mass that finally caused our jeep to slip to one side and hopelessly bog itself down. So, there was only one thing to do. We walked.

"The sun had been shining brightly in the valley far below, and none of us had brought a raincoat. . . . Now, as the rain poured down, we were soaked to the skin almost at once.

"Finally I saw up ahead the little shacks of the mountain village toward which we were headed, and soon we were welcomed into the little bamboo house-on-stilts that serves both as home for Pastor Ba Aye and his little family and also as the 'church' for the little congregation that meets to worship Christ up there on Elephant Mountain."

Ba Aye has been serving his congregation for five years. He himself was brought to Christ by Dr. William Hackett, Baptist missionary to Burma. In the five years that Ba Aye has been trudging through the mountains, he has made only six converts.

"Five long years of trudging those wearisome mountain trails," wrote Mr. Ward. "Five years of faithfully, earnestly preaching the Word of God . . . five years of visiting from house to house. . . . And five years, too, of misunderstanding and opposition and even persecution. Five years of seeing people *almost* come to Christ—but then fading away because of the opposition and the threats.

"There have been times of deep discouragement, times when Ba Aye has felt that he just couldn't go on. This last year in particular has brought many such trials and temptations, and he told me about them as we squatted there together around the fire in his bamboo house.

"Yes, he admitted, there have been those times this past year when he was about ready to give up—to look for an easier field of service. But then, late at night, while his family slept on the floor nearby, Ba Aye would sit and look into the fire even as he was doing now with me. And as he did, his mind would go back to last summer.

"Ba Aye was one of more than 500 pastors who attended the Pastors' Conference in Rangoon.

"He would remember the messages he heard at Rangoon, and he'd begin to straighten up as he recalled those hours of challenge and inspiration.

"He'd remember the other pastors who had come, those from all parts of Burma and from many different denominations, and suddenly he would begin to realize that even though he was serving Christ in this forgotten village on a remote mountain peak—he was part of the world-wide army of God that marches on to His Glory all around the globe. . . .

"And when he remembered the other pastors, Ba Aye told me, he would recall that they too had problems, that they too often faced defeat and discouragement, that their families also often had to do without. He remembered those nights in Rangoon when, the conference sessions over, the pastors had sat and talked and prayed and shared one another's burdens 'to thus fulfill the law of Christ.'

"Suddenly, he would find himself praying for this one and that. And when he prayed for them, his own problems grew smaller and smaller until finally they all but disappeared. . . ."

The inspiration that Ba Aye drew from the 1958 pastors' conference in Rangoon has been duplicated in the lives of 20,-000 pastors all over Asia. Since 1953, World Vision has conducted these conferences in Japan, Korea, Indonesia, Barbados, B.W.I., the Philippines, Thailand, Formosa, Vietnam, Malaya and Singapore, Burma, India, Ghana, and Colombia.

Their importance lies in the fact that there simply are not

enough missionaries to do the work that must be done. Countries like Korea and Formosa, where the percentage of Christians is relatively high, are the exceptions. One hundred years of missionary activity in Japan had brought only one-tenth of one per cent of people to Christ. In India, with its estimated population of 390,000,000, only about 10,000,000 belong to any branch of the Christian Church.

"If Asia is to be won for Christ, it must be won by Asians," Bob Pierce has said, time and again.

Larry Ward has added: "All thinking Christians today will agree with the truth of that assertion. Missionary enterprise in 1959 highlights the role of the Christian national worker who can so effectively reach his own people—and that does not in the least detract from the spiritual responsibility of the missionary himself.

"All too often, in days gone by, the Asian Christian worker on the grass roots level, the one who most desperately needs help, has worked under great handicaps. His income usually has been pitifully small. His social standing does not begin to compare with that of a minister in the United States or Canada. His fellowship is sometimes limited to virtually the members of his own family, and rarely reaches beyond his own parish or outside his particular denomination. Christian leaders in Asia—denominational officials and church council officials—have often been brought together for important conferences, but the local pastor too often has been overlooked. Yet in many respects he is much more important than the 'big' leaders."

There is another important reason why the conferences are necessary, Bob told me. "One by one, the countries of Asia are being closed to missionaries. Even countries that have not been taken over by Communists are beginning to impose restrictions. In July 1959, the Burmese government announced that the number of Protestant and Roman Catholic missionaries permitted to enter would be based on the pre-World War II number, and that no additional ones would be tolerated. Simultaneously, the government stated that all missionaries would be encouraged to engage primarily in humanitarian activities and to place evangelization in the hands of native personnel."

The conferences are conducted simply and efficiently, without elaborate ceremonies or heraldry. As much as a year in advance, the national pastors (with some assistance from World Vision field men) make the arrangements—they hire a hall, arrange for living quarters, and see that invitations are delivered to every pastor or evangelist in the country, no matter how remote his station may be. The committee not only provides funds for travel, but also attempts to make traveling as easy for the pastors as it can (in Thailand, for example, the executive group secured half-fare rates for pastors on the railroad), but there are many hundreds who experience difficulty in getting to the scene. A huge percentage of the ministers must walk, often for weeks. A day or two before the conference is to begin, the World Vision group arrives. The team usually includes Bob Pierce, Dr. Paul Rees, Dr. Richard C. Halverson, Dr. Carl F. H. Henry, Dr. Bernard Ramm, Larry Ward, and the Reverend Ellsworth Culver. They are joined by experienced pastors from other Asiatic countries—Bishop Sobrepena of United Church of Christ of the Philippines, Bishop Alexander Mar Theophilus of the Mar Thoma Church in India, plus a battery of experienced interpreters. Dr. Kyung Chik Han, pastor of the Young Nak Presbyterian Church in Seoul, Korea (the largest Presbyterian church in the Orient). All have participated several years. The men strip off their coats and get to work at once—conducting services, teaching Bible classes, discussing practical problems of the evangelist and missionary, exchanging experiences and, of course, praying. The delegates participate as actively as the leaders.

The meaning and significance of these meetings to the pastors who attend cannot be calculated. In Malaya, a minister from South India confessed to Dr. Paul Rees that he had been extremely bitter because his bishop had ordered him to stay on at his post for three years while his family went elsewhere for the children's education. At the conference, he said, he had felt ashamed of his bitterness. "Through prayer and fellowship with other brethren," says Dr. Rees, "he had been completely relieved of his bitterness and returned to his people full of joy and blessing." A missionary at the same meeting told Dr. Rees that he had been on the verge of giving up his work because of the loneliness and privation of his station, but the conference had met his need and he was determined to stay on.

The response of the national pastors to the conferences during the past few years continues to astonish the World Vision leaders. In Thailand, Pastor Taeyong had told Bob Pierce that he expected around 200 people, perhaps more. As it turned out, 350 registered for the meetings, and between 400 and 500 people attended each evening session.

"The overwhelming attendance of the pastors gave evidence to the great urgency for unity and determination in evangelizing Asia within the shortest possible time," Dr. Richard C. Halverson said afterward.

The most eloquent testimonials to the value of the conferences come from the pastors themselves. The Reverend Pai Kee Joo, of Korea, said after attending one:

"As I am always teaching the Word of God at church there

was hardly any chance to think on my situation and responsibility with deep meditation. But at every Conference I began to find my weak point as well as my lack of faithfulness. Especially I am confessing my unfaithfulness as a pastor to church members. Now I am renewing my decision for Christ, and reassuring the importance of my position in this meeting.

Another pastor later wrote, "By participating, I got the following: (1) I felt the powerfulness of Christ working among His people, (2) I got the loyalty to the work of God, (3) I wanted to show the great blessing I received to the unbeliever, and (4) finally I was feeding on my true spiritual food. . . ."

Letters of this kind come into the World Vision headquarters every day. The English in which they are written makes them all the more meaningful to the staff; by striving to express themselves in an alien tongue, the pastors are showing the depth of their feeling. One, from a pastor in Korea, sums up the feelings of all:

"At the opening service of the Conference, with so much joy and thrilling, I prayed and sang in tear," he wrote. "Throughout this meeting I received abundant grace, greater than ever before. I came to the meeting with tired mind, but went back home with vivid strength given by the Holy Spirit."

FEBRUARY 10 § CALCUTTA

As we drive into Calcutta from the airport, we pass many groups of people carrying large, elaborately carved figures of an idol, and in a number of vacant lots we see pavilions being erected.

"This is the feast of Saraswati," Bob says. "They call those tentlike things *pandals*. Saraswati is the goddess of Learning. All over the city, the people erect shrines to her and put up idols, and either tonight or tomorrow they will gather for the festival. Each neighborhood or group of people tries to outdo the other in decorating the shrines. Some of them get to be pretty elaborate."

Groups of students are hurrying along with their goddesses mounted on bicycles, rickshas, and carts. In no other Indian festival, I later learn, do the children and young people take such an enthusiastic part. Everywhere there are young girls in bright yellow saris, obviously worn just for this occasion.

"The worshiping goes on in the mornings," Bob says. "Then, in the evenings, there will be feasts in nearly all the schools and all the houses. At night on the last day of the festival—they call it a *puja*—they all take their goddesses down to the river and throw them in."

Public-address systems have been mounted on each pandal, and the strange music jangles through every block, clashing with the beating of drums and the sound of trumpets, all but drowning out the fierce cries of the multitudes of crows—

huge, blue-black birds, twice the size of the ones I see around my home—that seem to fill the sky, swarming over the telegraph poles and the roofs, drenching the sidewalks, and the people on them, with their white droppings.

Each time our bus stops for a traffic light, beggars leave the sidewalk and come to the side of the vehicle, staring up at us supplicatingly, their eyes wet with appeal, their palms reaching upward. Some are women with children, others are toothless old men, bent over with age and disease. They increase in number as we get nearer and nearer to the center of the city. So does the heat—and the foul conglomeration of odors. The streets seem to be covered with excrement, and the gutters are awash with urine; a white, humped cow, standing squarely in the path of our bus, calmly allows its bowels to move. Our driver waits until it is finished.

After nearly an hour and a half we finally reach the Great Eastern Hotel, reputedly Calcutta's finest. As soon we get off the bus, we are beset by a horde of chattering, ragged, bright-eyed little boys carrying shoeshine boxes, cans of polish, and dressed in filthy clothes. "Soosine? Soosine? One anna! One anna! Soosine, mister?" they clamor, tugging at our sleeves, our coats, surrounding us so that it is impossible to move. A stocky, dark-haired man with horn-rimmed glasses on the face of a scholar, appears and waves them all away. This is the Reverend Mr. Walter A. Corlett, pastor of Carey Baptist Church, an old friend of Bob's. They greet each other warmly, and as I shake hands with Mr. Corlett and see his forthright, brisk manner which is nevertheless warm, I decide at once that he is a man worth having for a friend. He is British; although he has been in India for thirty years, his accent is still strong. He tells us that it was impossible to get us into the Great Eastern; he has put us in Spence's Hotel, two blocks away. Bob and Reinhold and I walk there, hastening to get away from the nagging, badgering shoeshine boys. Spence's is located at the end of an alley. Men are living on the sidewalks in this alley; some are cobblers, others hire themselves out as messengers, one is a tailor. Automatically, as we pass, the beggars stretch out their hands and utter the whining nasal sound—"*Aaanh, aaanh!*" that later comes to echo in my mind as the most typical noise in this country of inconceivable overcrowding, dirt and poverty.

Nothing in our previous experience has prepared us for the room in which we are quartered in Spence's. The lobby itself gives no warning. It is small, and equipped with two desks, one for the clerk, set in an alcove, and one standing in the center of the lobby for the hall porter. There are travel posters on the wall, and a sign that says there is a bar and a restaurant; except for the eight white-robed porters who cluster about us, it could be a small hotel in England, in Bristol, perhaps, or Leicester. Just behind the lobby is the elevator, which is old but creakily serviceable. We follow the herd of porters down a long, dank corridor, and come at last to our room.

The head porter opens the door with a flourish and a bow. Our eyes grow large. The room has ceilings about twenty-five feet high and a mosaic-tile floor. It is dark and cavernous; two unfrosted glass incandescent bulbs hang on twelve-foot cords from the ceiling, each about twenty-five watts in strength. There are three single beds, side by side. The furniture is massive old English, the upholstering torn and patched, the stuffing coming out here and there. The bathroom was put in at least fifty years ago, and has not been changed. There are flies everywhere, clustering about the naked light bulbs, crawling about over the furniture.

"Welcome to the Calcutta Boys' Club," Bob says. "They

had to put the three of us in one room because they're so crowded."

The porters are busy dropping our bags on the tile floor. One plunks down Reinhold's camera case as though it were a sack of old clothes. Reinhold closes his eyes.

We are to meet Walter Corlett for dinner, later. Now we putter about, partially unpacking, placing suitcases and bags in various shadows of the dingy room. There is a single window, but it is nailed tight and covered with a shutter—to keep out the heat, presumably. I sit and write my wife: "India is hard to believe. No pictures I ever have seen have done justice to the filth, the stench, the poverty. The people lie by the sides of the road in mud; they squat in gutters, huddle together in window sills. They are dressed in scraps of grimy rags; dirt is encrusted a half-inch thick on their feet. Women with horrible open sores walk along carrying babies obviously suffering from malnutrition. In Hong Kong and Thailand we saw ten- and twelve-year-old boys running elevators, waiting on tables, and the like, but here there are six- and seven-year-olds doing everything but pulling pedicabs. Flies everywhere. People eating from bowls in which flies have drowned or suffocated. . . ."

An hour later the three of us return to the Great Eastern to keep an appointment with Walter Corlett.

"I've asked Miss Barbara Best to join with us," Walter tells Bob.

"Good, good, I've always wanted to meet her—I've known about her work for years," Bob says.

While we wait for her in the lobby, Walter tells me of Miss Best's work with an interdenominational mission called the Nepal Evangelistic Band, at Pokhra, the capital of Nepal. "They were the first Christians into that country," he says.

"For fifteen years, Miss Best and a Dr. Lily O'Hanlon kept on working on the Indian side of the Nepal border, and finally their efforts were blessed. They were invited into the country to set up missions. By then they had a group of Nepalese converts who agreed to go into the interior with them. They found an excellent site near the Annapurna mass of mountains and set up a hospital there. It was, and is today, a faith mission entirely dependent upon the giving of God's people. They—the Nepalese—call it the Shining Hospital because it is made of sectional huts of aluminum. It's difficult to describe the almost unbelievable hardship these women endure in doing the Lord's work. You'd better let her tell you about it."

A tall, frail woman with kindly dark eyes behind spectacles, her hair parted neatly in the middle like that of a schoolteacher, approaches us. After Walter introduces us, Miss Best speaks of the work in Nepal as though it were commonplace. She is going back there soon, she tells us; another project that she has been working on in Gorakhpur is all but finished. She came first to India from Somerset, England, her home, twenty-five years ago, spent thirteen years in India, went to Uganda for eight years, then went back to England to live in retirement with her brother. The call was too strong for her to resist. She came back in 1957, and one can tell, by listening to her, that it may be a long time before she sees England again.

"Dr. O'Hanlon's work at Shining Hospital," she tells us, "was begun by Dr. Kitty Harboard, who went up there and lived in a house on the border. She and Dr. O'Hanlon found a great deal of leprosy and tuberculosis, and many natives walking around with horrible burns. They would be burned in village fires and had no method of taking care of themselves. In the beginning, they worked with burn cases as well as they could, applying salves and unguents, but today, there is a doctor at Shining Hospital, Ruth Watson, who can do skin grafts.

"It is not really the most favorable place in the world in which to live," Miss Best says, with a slight smile. "It is very cold, for one thing . . . the wind comes straight from the snows of Tibet. It is hard to grow food, although we do what we can. The lepers help us with crops . . . last year, we raised grain: millet, maize, buckwheat, and lentils. We get meat about once every fortnight. Goat, mainly. We make our own bread from rice flour. Sugar and tea are sent to us by friends. Vegetables are our main problem because there is such a scarcity of water."

"I wish you'd tell these men about the water," Walter Corlett says.

"Shining Hospital is on a cliff, with a river below," Miss Best says. "The cliff is three hundred feet high, and water had to be carried up it from a spring near the river below. The river is full of glacial sediment and therefore its water cannot be used. But last year we dug a channel to divert some of the treacherous current, and now we use hydraulic power to lift up our spring water. The equipment is very primitive. If we had more modern equipment we might devote less of our time to getting the water supply and more to help the people who need help."

Reinhold nudges me. With his chin, he indicates Bob. I find Bob listening intently. The determination is plain on his face.

"How many patients up there, Miss Best?" he asks.

"There are twenty-four inpatients at Shining Hospital. But we treat anyone who comes to us. Some have come, been cured, and still stay on. Lepers, as of course you already know, seldom return to their homes. We trek around the villages and ask the leaders to please take back lepers who come with a certificate from us saying they're cured, but we've only had one taken back."

"What about teaching the Word of Christ?"

"At the Shining Hospital, there are about sixty native Christians," she says. "We are very encouraged. The mountaineers constantly come down for teaching. The Nepalese government hasn't bothered us in Pokhra—that is, it has not prohibited the teaching of Christianity. But back on the border, some time ago, one man was put in jail for baptizing. We believe they've let us alone because as yet we're so small, we can't seem to be a threat."

Bob's face is still full of concern and resolve. As though I had been bidden to give him a cue, I say, "How did you say you are supported, Miss Best?"

"We get it in answer to prayer. That seems to be the way God does His work."

"What keeps you there?"

She is genuinely surprised at the question. "Why, there is a partnership with God there, sir. Only that could keep a person in a place like Pokhra. It is the willing of God and the enabling of God." This last sentence is uttered quietly.

"Walter," Bob says, as I have almost known that he would, "I wonder if World Vision couldn't do something for these ladies?"

That was the end of our conversation, but it was only the beginning of Bob's practical interest. A few months after I had returned to the United States I had a letter from Walter Corlett. He gave me recent news of the Shining Hospital: "So far I have received $600 from W. V. to bring water from the 300-foot-deep ravine. We will need much more before we can complete this project, but this is a magnificent beginning."

FEBRUARY 11 § NEW DELHI

In order to get visas to visit Assam, we have come to the Indian capital. Two men are waiting for us there—the Reverend Clifton Robinson, who has been in New Delhi for years, knows the officials, and feels he can help us set our visas, and a friend of his, the Reverend Clarence Sekerak, of the First Friends Church, Park and Broadway, in Alliance, Ohio. Robinson is a bluff, hearty, brisk man with dark hair, a cordial smile and a distinct resemblance to Jonathan Winters, the comedian. Sekerak is blond, lean, and affable. Robinson has his own church in New Delhi. Sekerak has been out with the Youth For Christ team for the tenth annual Congress for Christian Youth, and he is proceeding on around the world.

Coming in from the airport, we pass the United States Embassy, the new building designed by Edward Stone, which has received much publicity in the States. It is indeed beautiful, a light and airy, lacy structure that looks as though it would be cool within. But the setting in which it sits leaves a good deal to be desired. None of the grounds yet have been landscaped, and on either side are parked hundreds of military vehicles that look as though they have been abandoned. Again I note that our State Department has been up to its old trick of presenting only part of a foreign picture to those of us who cannot travel; all pictures of the new building distributed in the States showed only the building itself, and not the ugly surroundings. Nearby, Mr. Robinson points out the new Russian Embassy, in the process of being completed. "It's going to be a much more imposing structure than ours," he says ruefully.

"Our people don't realize it at home," Bob says, "but the Communists are beating us out in most of these countries out here." He cast his eyes upward. "O Lord, I wish there were some way of waking our people up. In some places, the pastors' conferences we sponsor are the only weapons the United States has. I'm convinced of that. It's the only way we can get to the native leaders and show them what democracy is all about."

We arrive at the home of an official Mr. Robinson knows, a lady equipped to cut through the webs of red tape on which the Indian government seems, to an outsider, to thrive.

Reinhold and I and Mr. Sekerak wait in the automobile while the two ministers are conferring in the house with the lady official, listening to the incessant bawling and swooping of the jungle crows; they seem to be more numerous than the people. Across the street, under a tree, an itinerant barber is cutting a customer's hair. Mr. Sekerak tells us about a missionary hospital he recently visited near Madras, operated by Friends. Founded in 1895, the hospital has been running ever since, but only during the past few years has the staff begun to transfer responsibility to Indian personnel. "Oh, it's a long, long struggle out here," he says, but his tone is not despairing. "I thank God I've been given the privilege of coming out to see how great the burden really is. The people I've met! The stories I've heard! Last week I was visiting the American Baptist Mission in Rangoon, Burma, and I had a chance for some fellowship with the Reverend Mr. Don Crider, a missionary from Altoona, Pennsylvania. He told me an incident that challenged my heart. Assam, where you fellows are trying to go, is one of the fourteen Indian states, and, as you know, it borders on Burma. The people there are very primitive. Many of them used to be head-hunters. In 1954, in Rangoon, the Burmese Baptists heard an urgent appeal for Christian workers, Labwi Htingnan, a layman, at that time headmaster of a Burmese government school, offered to go. He was thirty-seven and had a family of seven children. Still, he went. He ended up at the Hurowng Valley, at the village of Shingbwiyang. He cleared a place in the jungle and started a school. The dialect spoken there was called Naga. It was new to Labwi, but he tackled it and he learned it. Within seven months the work had progressed so well that they were ready for the ordination of the first deacons. Eleven Assamese were baptized. The church was formed and put into operation—and all because one layman felt the urge to go and do missionary work!"

After nearly an hour, Bob and Mr. Robinson came from the house. Bob's slouching walk tells me that he is disappointed. We must go to the visa bureau, he says, after lunch —but first we must go to Mr. Robinson's house and wait for a call telling us when and where to go. Mr. Robinson and his wife have a lunch waiting. Like all missionaries' wives, she is eager for news from the States, and of other missionaries. Again it comes home to me that missionaries actually constitute a close-knit fraternity, as though the love of God and the joy in His work has bound them even to kindred souls they do not know and possibly may never see. Somehow, all of them know vaguely of each other's activities.

Mrs. Robinson turns out to be a fine cook, and Reinhold and I, starved after our grapplings with the meager fare we found in Calcutta, willingly pass our plates for second helpings. After lunch we wait for the telephone call. An hour passes; it does not come. Reinhold and I go out for a walk with the Robinsons' teen-age daughter, who volunteers to show us the Humayun Tomb, which is nearby. The tomb is considered to rank with the Taj Mahal, and has been almost completely restored. Outside its entrance gate is an enterprising man behind a stand, with a voice like jungle crows asking us to buy his post cards and souvenirs; and just inside the gate stands the inevitable beggar, thin and ghostly, more like an old woman than a man.

"Am poor *bland* man," he chants (someone has taught him the English phrases he needs for his trade). "*Bland* man, cannot *seeeeee*, very *poor*." He clutches his finger bones together and bows his head and opens the lids of his sightless eyes, and as I look at him I cannot help but reflect that the money the government spent to restore this place of the dead might have been better spent in providing food and shelter for this blind beggar and the millions like him. The beggar has spoiled my interest in the tomb; it is impossible for me to marvel at the wonders of the past while reflecting upon a government, a culture, indeed a religion, that permits its blind and crippled and destitute to live in squalor that must be seen to be believed. Again I appreciate Bob Pierce's zeal: part of his mission is to instill a respect for human life, for human dignity, which seems to me, visiting it for the first time, so strikingly lacking in this nation.

From the Humayun Tomb we go to an abandoned Moslem cemetery near the Robinsons' house. Those who once cared for it have long since gone to Pakistan, to be with their fellows; now beggars and servants-of-servants are living in the marble chambers of the deceased. An old man and a goat, both panting in the sun, seek the skimpy shelter of a tree. Four

men, their palms extended, offer to show us around the graveyard colony. We go with them, which is pointless, for none
can speak English. Children peer at us timorously from the
marble doorways of the tombs, venture out and follow us. A
legless man drags himself along through the dust with his
hands, calling out his woes, which are his wares. The one
bright spot in this dismal tour of sight-seeing is the sight of
a man leading a trained bear, which rears to his hind legs immediately upon confronting us. At first we conclude that the
bear has been taught to do his dance the instant a potential
audience comes into view. Then we see the stick, and its sharp
iron goad, with which his master prods him. We go back to
the house.

The call has not come. Bob and Mr. Robinson decide that
we will go on to the passport bureau and see what will happen there. By now I am certain that we are not going to get
the visas we seek, and I am right. After the eighth or ninth
official has told Bob and Mr. Robinson that he knows nothing
of our applications, we check into a hotel. A call comes for
us there: it is possible, says some mysterious civil servant, that
our visas will be issued the next day. *Just* possible, he emphasizes.

The hotel is the Ashoka, out in the area in which our Embassy sits, some five miles from the city proper. Our room
overlooks a village of mud huts, where servants-of-servants
live. Reinhold takes some pictures there the next morning,
as we stroll through the single street. I wonder what these
people, whose daily single meal is a kind of stew made of ran-
cid goat meat and wilted vegetables, must think as they look
up at the towering Ashoka and regard (seemingly without
rancor) our Western shirts and trousers, meanwhile pulling
their own rags about them to keep off the blistering sun. As

this thought occurs to me I begin to understand something of the Indian civil servant's attitude toward foreigners. The civil servant has raised himself to a station far above that of the masses, but he cannot get them out of his conscience. Therefore he cannot help his indignation. Nor can he be blamed, in this fearful heat, for his incompetence and his perpetual brusqueness. Yet it is a test for the Westerner who must deal with him, and one that must make each missionary call upon all his patience and forbearance in order to communicate the love of God that sustains him.

When Reinhold and I return to the hotel we find a note from Bob. He and Mr. Robinson have gone to see yet another official. While we are waiting I call our Embassy and, after much difficulty, finally get through to a man whose name I was given in the States, a man with whom I have some mutual friends. He comes to the hotel a little later for a talk. He is extremely busy—that is plain; he is attached to our Ambassador's personal staff. In the course of our conversation I happen to ask him if he has been studying the language.

"Lord, no!" he cries, in horror. "I'd never have time for that. And besides, where would I start? There are over four hundred main dialects, don't forget, and dialects of those dialects. Besides, English is spoken everywhere here—it's the lingua franca."

The picture of Sam Moffett, sitting with his wife in a dirty village in Korea, slowly and painstakingly learning the language so that he may carry on his work, comes to my mind.

"I mean," the man from our Ambassador's office says, defensively, "we've got enough to do without bothering with the language."

"The missionaries learn the languages of the people they work with," I say.

"Missionaries," he says contemptuously.

Our fellowship with this fellow ends soon after this brief exchange. He makes his excuses. He is very, very busy, he emphasizes again; he must get back to the Embassy. We promise to give his regards to friends in the States.

Bob comes back. Before he speaks, I sense his disappointment. "There is trouble on the borders among the tribes," he says. "They have to check into us before they grant our visas. It's too bad. I did so want you fellows to meet Rochunga and hear his story. I wanted you to see what he's doing up there in Assam. Maybe some other time."

On the plane going back to Calcutta I tell Bob of our conversation with the Ambassador's man.

"I know, I know," he says. "It's like that in many, many cases. They just can't take the time to learn the language, and they never get as close to the people as they ought to get."

FEBRUARY 13 § CALCUTTA

Heat. Blistering, withering, wilting heat. Reinhold is in transports. "What glorious weather!" he shouts, ducking a shoe I scale at him. We have moved from our luxurious quarters in Spence's Hotel to a slightly cooler room in the Great Eastern, but the air is still stifling and we are soaked by our own sweat.

The afternoon minutes tick by. The heat continues to press in. Teatime comes. The waiter brings in a tray laden with oily liquid in a pot, damp sandwiches, and flies. I am ready to tell him to take it all away when, quite suddenly, a remarkable feeling takes hold of me. I think of Bob Pierce and his reactions to hardship, to frustration, even to danger, all of which we have experienced on this trip. Bob is not without temperament. I have seen him lose his temper; once, when we were rushing to catch a plane, a hotel clerk took a fearfully long time to give us the bill, and Bob spoke to him sharply. Yet his faith, his enduring awareness of the teachings of Christ, enable him to get through many things that would—to use an old phrase of my father's—make a preacher swear.

A knock sounds at the door. We yell, "Come in," and Walter Corlett enters. "Rochunga is here," he says.

Rochunga Pudaite, the young man we were to have seen in Assam, has flown down to see us because we could not get up to see him. We shake hands. He is in his early thirties, a slender man of medium height with shining black hair and regular features, but it is not his physical appearance that arrests the attention. It is, rather, the joy that fairly shines out of his eyes. I sense immediately that this man has found an inner peace that has made him both brave and resolute. "We were so sorry you could not come up to Assam," he says. "Villagers had been coming from other places for days— some walked a hundred miles just to see Dr. Bob, and we had made preparations to kill and roast three cows, one for each of you."

"Bless your heart, Rochunga," says Bob, who also has come in. "Yes, we're disappointed. I wanted these men to see for themselves what you are doing up there."

Rochunga takes off his coat, folds it neatly, and places it over the back of a chair. I learn later that it is the only suit he owns. Over a cup of tea, he begins to talk.

Rochunga Pudaite was born on December 4, 1927, in the

state of Manipur, in Assam, in a village called Senvon. To-day, as when he was a child, Senvon has a population of around 2000. "There are not many houses in the village—only about four hundred," Rochunga explains, "because when a son gets married he usually moves his wife into the house of his father." The tribe in this village is called the Hmar, and its origins are obscure. "Our traditional poetry," says Rochunga, "says that we come from Shen State, in Burma. I believe the ancestors were fleeing from the Mongols and gradually migrated to the west, then across the border from Burma into Assam. That was many, many years ago. From the poetry I also gather that they migrated for two reasons —occasional famine and hostility from neighboring tribes."

Before the British entered that part of India, Rochunga's paternal grandfather had been a chief. The British took over Assam in 1871, and from then on the natives were in almost continual trouble. "Our people fought against the British directly and indirectly," Rochunga continues. Yes, he adds, they were head-hunters; or so the British labeled them. He does not say if they were or were not head-hunters, and I hesitate to pin him down on this point. It is possible to conclude that they might not have been head-hunters if they had not been pressured into it.

"My grandfather," says Rochunga, "went into hiding when the British came. He could not stand the invasion. He did not go away. He went into hiding in his own village, and did not make himself known."

Rochunga pauses. "My father's name was Changwa," he says. "Back in 1910 he made a decision for Christ. I don't know how old he was then. I believe he may have been about fourteen. We never had any way of recording his age, so we don't know how old he really is." He pauses again, obviously troubled. "Perhaps," he says, hesitantly, "I ought to start at the very beginning, with the man who led my father to Christ."

The man's name was Watkin R. Roberts. He was a Presbyterian, who around the turn of the century was the medical assistant to a Dr. Frasier, who was a district medical officer at Caernarvon, Wales, and who came out to India under the auspices of the Welsh Missionary Society. Frasier and Roberts first went into the Lushai Hills, where they learned the language of the people and then determined to go on with their work in other areas where other tribes were. "Though only a medical assistant," says Rochunga, "Watkin Roberts had a great challenge for places where the gospel had not entered. He felt that the greatest thing he could do would be to give them the language of the gospel, the literature."

One of the places Roberts felt he should go was the village where Rochunga's grandfather had been chief. No one could visit that village without a permit. Other areas also were closed. Roberts then did the next best thing. He went back to Calcutta and made his wishes known to Christians there. Someone gave him twenty-five rupees, and with that money he started a small bookstore called Evangelical Literature Truck.

"He began to inquire about different tribal chiefs," says Rochunga. "He got the names of most of them, and he began sending gospels up from Calcutta into the Lushai Hills. The gospel of St. John somehow fell into the hands of the chief of Senvon, the one the British had put in as head. Now, Watkin Roberts had written in the back, 'For further information, communicate with So-and-So.' Himself. The chief did not have a piece of paper, but he tore out the flyleaf of the gospel and he wrote on the back:

" 'Please, sir, can you come yourself?'

"You see, he had read it all over and over and was so impressed that he felt he must talk to the man who sent it out into the Lushai Hills."

At this point I ask about the native religion of the Lushai Hills.

"It is hard to explain. They worshiped a great, far-off evil spirit, and a god called Khuonu, a female god, the mother of creation . . . and this god never did any harm. They believed in life after death, not quite like the migration of a soul, but they talked about a soul going into the moon or stars, and they believed that for six months after death the spirit of the dead kept visiting the grave, and after that it turned into something like a bee and flew away. . . .

"And every new moon for six months the mother, or father, or head of the family would go to the grave and offer something for the spirit to eat. Sometimes a crow would eat it, or another bird, or the rains would wash it away, and then they would feel very happy because the spirit had been fed.

"I guess you would call it sort of an animism. They worshiped the sun, the moon, a big tree, a big rock, or a small river. They worshiped anything that was big. If it was big the god had to be in it. And they all would offer sacrifices."

Rochunga's face is at once grave and humorous as he tells of the religion, which was the religion of his grandparents and, for a time, his parents as well.

"Watkin Roberts decided to go into the Lushai Hills as soon as he got the flyleaf," Rochunga goes on. "He had to have a special permit to go up there, and he went to the British officer in charge of the area. The officer said, 'You can't possibly go into that section without at least one hundred and fifty soldiers. Those natives are dangerous.' Roberts said, 'But I have this call. I *must* go.' A little later, the officer called the commander of the Assam Rifles to see if he could send some soldiers with the missionary. They laughed at the idea. 'Even if we would send soldiers with a missionary,' they said, 'we have none to spare.'

"And Watkin Roberts said, 'Who am I not to obey the voice of God?' And he determined that he would come. When the British officer saw how he felt, he asked him to sign a document promising that in the event he lost his life the British government would not be held responsible. He promised that he would travel at his own risk, and he prayed and asked God to give him guidance.

"His prayers were answered. That same evening, a young man by the name of Dala, who knew the language of our people, came to Watkin Roberts and said, 'I am here in search of education, and if you teach me I will go with you and be your guide and interpreter.'

" 'I have no money to pay you,' Watkin Roberts said. 'But if you have confidence in my God, I will take you.' Dala was converted before the end of the trip.

"Then another miraculous thing happened. Three or four young men appeared before Watkin Roberts and said, 'We hear that you offered education to Dala, and if you will take us with you and educate us, we will be your bodyguard.'

"After a few days, they left. They did not know the proper way to go, and so they took a long route. It should have been only one hundred and twenty miles, but they walked over two hundred miles into the mountains. And to their great surprise, they were greeted not by dangerous head-hunters, but by hundreds and hundreds of people all bearing gifts.

"This took place on February 14, 1910. Watkin Roberts

stayed six days. On the first day he preached the gospel. On the second and succeeding days he talked to the chiefs and the elders, hoping to convert them, but he could not reach their hearts.

"On the fifth evening he went out, exasperated with himself and his efforts, and prayed and prayed for guidance.

"Then Dala, the translator, had an idea. He said to Watkin Roberts, 'Among the tribes, when they have a war, and peace comes, they cannot write with pen and paper the agreement that settles it, because they do not know how. But the two chiefs involved in the war will come together on the boundary between their territories and kill a peace offering, a pig or a cow, and while the blood of the animal is flowing the chief will touch the animal on the side and the other will speak the terms of their peace, and if the terms are agreed upon the broken relationship is whole again.'

"And Watkin Roberts thought: If I put it into those terms, those words that they can understand, perhaps that will bring them to God.

"He went to the chiefs and said, 'My brothers, you have been at war with God. There has been no peace, nothing but trouble and turmoil. But God so loved the world that He sent His only begotten Son to die on the boundary in Calvary. This time it is not the blood of a bull or a pig, but the blood of God's son, sent to you for redemption.' And in that way he offered the whole story of redemption, and the chief himself and all the elders accepted the Lord that day. And Watkin Roberts left that day and never went back, but what he accomplished there will always remain."

Rochunga pauses. His expression is that of a man contemplating a profundity.

"The Word of God remained," he says. "Among those

who heard it was my father, and he wanted to know more. He went to Aijal, the capital, to read the Bible they had there because he could not buy one of his own. It was one hundred twenty miles, and he walked. It is hard walking through those jungle hills, and there are beasts on every side, and snakes, but I tell you, there was the fire of God in my father. He had a great determination, and he wanted to preach. He wanted to learn so that he could preach.

"My grandfather, the old chief, was still in hiding in the village, and he was displeased when my father told him about the Word of God. He threw him out of the house, saying, 'You will be eaten up by wild beasts.' My father said, 'I must tell everyone about the feeling of joy in me since I have found Christ,' and still my grandfather threw him out to the tigers and the bears. And do you know? A few days after that happened, my grandfather, who had been a very famous hunter among his people, actually was torn to pieces by a bear. It makes me think."

Rochunga's father, Changwa, from then on became an itinerant preacher, trudging hundreds of miles through the jungle. Sometimes he would be gone from his village more than a year. To help support himself, he bought an old sewing machine and acted as a tailor for people he met, and while he was mending clothes he would preach. In the evenings he would hold meetings. He married in 1920, and his wife bore him two sons, Ramlien and Rochunga. Ramlien currently is helping with various tribes in the area, and translating the Bible into the language of the Simta people.

"Tell us about your mother, Rochunga," Walter Corlett says.

"Yes, that is a story," Rochunga says. "My mother became an invalid when I was born. For years she never went out of the house. In 1933, my father heard a call to go to Rulphui and preach. He wanted to take his family with him, but he was afraid the trip would be too much for my mother. She said, 'If you must go, you must go,' and we began packing. Some of our friends in the village came to me and said, 'Your father must be mad—your mother cannot make such a journey.' I told this to my father and he told me not to mind what they said. 'It is God's will that we go,' he said. We started out the next morning, my father supporting my mother on the one side, and I helping to support her on the other. At the edge of the village she fell down in a faint. We thought she would die. We knelt down and prayed for her, and in a little while, as though a miracle had come to pass, she got up and started off. And the first day she walked eight miles. This was through very rough jungle. The next day she walked fifteen miles with us, without support. When we reached our destination, she was no longer an invalid any more—she was strong enough to serve tea to the bearers who had accompanied us. It was indeed a miracle."

Rochunga had begun his education in 1933, when he was six, and he kept on with it in Pulphui Village in a school run by some missionaries. "That school had no facilities for the state examinations," he says, "and so in order to take my first one I walked to Tinsuong Village. It was twenty-six miles, through the jungle." He did that each year until 1941, when he decided to go to Churachandpur Mission School. This institution was located ninety-six miles from his home. "I walked the distance four times a year," Rochunga says. "It was a rough road, because there was no road—again, all jungle." After graduating from this school, the equivalent of the American junior high school, he wanted to go on. His father had no money. Once more he set out on foot, walking eighty miles to Jorhat Christian High School. There he busied himself at odd jobs, sweeping out rooms, working as a gardener, putting up fences and doing other carpentry.

"My father's village, Pulphui, had no post office," Rochunga says. "He was eager to hear from me, to find out how my studies were coming . . . and the nearest place where he could get letters was eighty miles away. So he would walk there, and back, once each month. In 1953 I had an interview with Prime Minister Nehru, who was visiting a school where I was, and I told him my father had covered 6986 miles on foot to get my letters."

Rochunga stayed in Jorhat Christian High School, doing his small tasks and saving every cent he could, until 1949. He went to Calcutta and enrolled in St. Paul's College of the Anglican Church. After he had paid his admission fee he had five rupees—about one American dollar—left to his name. "That year was very hard," he says, "but I did get a scholarship from the government."

Bob Pierce met Rochunga on his first trip through India, in 1951. By then the young man had decided that he would go back to Assam to help his people, but he was determined to get as much education as possible. Bob raised money for him to go to Allahabad College in 1952. He graduated from there in 1954 and, still supported by World Vision, went to Scotland, to Glasgow Bible Training Institute. After a year he went on to Wheaton College, in Illinois, and took most of his work toward a Master of Arts degree. Then he returned to Assam, to Sielmat.

Currently Rochunga, his brother, and his father are working in a Bible school they have established which also supports a small clinic. About twenty people work in it full time, teaching and translating the Scriptures into native dialects, going out and preaching in the villages.

"Ninety per cent of the people in Sielmat are Christians," Rochunga says. "And over eighty per cent, now, in the entire Hmar tribe. I believe there are about eighty thousand all told, in our tribe."

Walter Corlett interposes, "Rochunga, his father and brother are doing a magnificent job up there."

"No," Rochunga says. "The name Rochunga means Inheritor of Highest Treasure." Then he stops, getting ready to say what we have heard so many times from our missionary friends: "I am not doing the work. God is."

FEBRUARY 19 § MARAMON

The history of the Mar Thoma Church goes back, it is said, to nine or twelve years after Christ was crucified, depending upon how one reckons time (a dispute I am not qualified to enter). It began when St. Thomas the Apostle traveled far east to the Indian city of Mouziris, a major seaport on the Malabar coast. According to tradition, that was in A.D. 52. Jews already had settled in the Cochin area (in Cochin today there is still a synagogue dating back to that time) and St. Thomas began preaching first to them and later to Hindus. "Through the ministry of the Word and the many miracles which tradition attributes to him, he brought many high-caste Hindus to the Christian faith," says the Most Reverend Juhanon Mar Thoma, the present Metropolitan of the Church, in his "Christianity in India and a Brief History of the Mar Thoma Syrian Church." In this pamphlet, published in 1952 and revised in 1954, the author admits that not much definite is known of St. Thomas' activities beyond the fact that he *did* preach. There are two conflicting stories as to how Thomas met his end. One says that after founding seven Christian churches in the Malabar area, he made his way northeast into the Madras section, where resentful Brahmins speared him to death. The second states that his death was accidental—a bowman, hunting with falcons, shot him. This second version says that his body was interred at Mylapore, and that his bones later were taken to Edessa. That too is open to question. Another variation holds that after the Christians left Mylapore, presumably driven out by the Hindus, the saint's resting place was forgotten. The Portuguese reached the city in the early sixteenth century, and a Mohammedan told them that the remains were buried in a chapel. They dug them up and sent them to Goa. But in Mylapore, in a reliquary in the San Thomé Church, there are still pieces of bone that allegedly are Thomas', and a sliver of the arrow, or spear, that may have killed him. Roman Catholics still make pilgrimages to this shrine. There is a third story which, at first inspection, seems more legendary than the first two, yet partially is supported by history. According to an apocryphal book of the third century, Acts of Thomas, when the Apostle landed he was taken by an agent to King Gundaphorus, an Indo-Parthian king. The agent told the King that Thomas was a carpenter, and the King gave him money to build him a palace. Thomas promptly took this money and gave it to the poor. When the King came to see his new dwelling, he was told that his real palace would be in the Kingdom of Heaven.

The King then threw both Thomas and the agent into prison to await execution. At about the same time, the King's brother became ill. He had been interested in the teachings of Thomas, and in a dream he imagined that he died and went to Heaven, where angels showed him the palace Thomas had built. He awoke, rushed to the King to tell him the dream, and secured the release of the two men. King Gundaphorus then became a Christian himself and sent Thomas out to preach in his dominion. Most scholars thought this story a legend until, in the late nineteenth century, excavations in the Punjab revealed that there actually had been an Indo-Parthian king named Gundaphorus who had lived in the middle of the first century and therefore had been a contemporary of St. Thomas.

Students of Christianity in India have devoted much time to arguing the merits of all these stories, but they are agreed that those who heard the gospel of St. Thomas spread it to others. Although there are no accurate or definite records, it is known that Christianity survived through the third century and began to expand in the middle of the fourth, with the visit of another Thomas, a Syrian merchant called Thomas of Cana, who was sent out to Malabar by the Catholicose of Jerusalem around A.D. 345. He and his retinue were welcomed in old Cranganore by the Rajah, who gave them a town to live in and accorded them certain social privileges. In the fourth century, many Christians were persecuted in Persia, and it is believed that many of them followed Thomas of Cana to Malabar. In the sixth century a merchant from Alexandria, Cosmas, known as The Indian Voyager, visited Malabar and later noted that the Christians there had a bishop from Persia ruling them. The church continued to exist during the following centuries, although it was subject to many migrations, attempted control by Roman Catholics, and disputes among its leaders. The present Mar Thoma Syrian Church is directly descended from the original ancient Syrian Church; as now constituted, it is reformed, and is 150 years old. It is one of the least-known branches of the Christian Church, but it is highly respected in Southern India, where the bulk of the Indian Christians live. There are now around 2,000,000 Christians in what can be termed the Malabar area. . . .

All this I have learned from Bob, from Walter Corlett, and from various ministers in the Mar Thoma Church during the past three days. The morning after our meeting with Rochunga, we left Calcutta for Madras, expecting to change planes there for the journey down to Cochin. At Madras we were bumped off our course; for some reason our reservations had not been confirmed. We spent the afternoon wandering around the city in rickshas, visiting temples; at one, we saw our first snake charmer, an old man in rags who carried two cobras in a tiny basket under his arm. Bob and Reinhold turned back early. I went on to the Madras Zoo, where I saw an African lion named, of all things, Nelson, and a tiger named John. In the morning there was one seat available on one southbound aircraft and two on another. Bob went ahead, and Reinhold and I followed in a couple of hours, flying in the Indian Airlines' rickety DC-3 from Madras to Tiruchirappali to Trivandrum to Cochin. Walter Corlett and Bob flew from Calcutta to Cochin before we came in, and the two of them went on from Cochin to the hamlet of Maramon, where the annual Maramon Convention, a huge mass meeting sponsored by the church, is being held. I am writing this at the convention itself. Reinhold and I came down this morning from Cochin, in a hired car that contrived to break down as soon as we were safely away from any possible chance of succor from the city. We had just come off a ferry—two canoes with a platform lashed to it—that took us across a river not more than fifty yards wide, and had plunged into the jungle when the engine gave two short coughing sounds and died. The driver, who spoke no English, leaped from his seat and immediately threw up the hood over the motor. He jumped up on the fender, then, and dived inside, chattering to himself. Fortunately, we had stopped under a tree on the outskirts of a village. There was some shade, but the heat was as challenging as it had been in Calcutta. All around were palms and heavy jungle ferns; squadrons of crows dived in and out among the trees, and we could hear the shrieks of monkeys and other animals. Flies and other insects came in hordes. Presently, out of the tangled greenery on both sides of the one-lane macadam road, skinny boys and men began to appear, moving in upon us silently to see what was happening. When they discovered that we were not Indians, they began to chatter excitedly to each other; they giggled and pointed and exchanged knowing nods. "Speak English?" Reinhold said to one. He smiled and shook his head energetically from left to right. Everyone laughed.

"This man hasn't the first idea of what's the matter with the motor," I said glumly.

"It's probably the carburetor," Reinhold said. "Something's clogged, probably."

The man had taken out a variety of parts and had spread them on the fender. The people from the jungle were picking them up, handing them back and forth, and—I felt certain—misplacing them. The driver paid no attention; he went on taking out parts. Presently he climbed out of the narrow space into which he had wedged himself and began looking at the parts he had removed. Up to this point, the authority of his movements had been fairly reassuring, despite my voiced doubts, but now he embarked upon a ritual that made me certain that we would never get started again. He picked up each small piece he had pulled out, wiped it with a cloth, licked it and sucked it.

Reinhold and I could only stare at each other.

"Let's try to thumb a ride back to Cochin and get another car," I said.

The crowd was watching the driver in obvious admiration. He paid no attention to them; he went on wiping, licking and sucking, and after he had finished with each part he smeared the grease away from his lips, frowned, and began fitting the parts together.

Within a half-hour we were on our way again. Behind us, the natives waved. Within another half-hour, we were confronted by the most shattering sight we have seen thus far. We had come to another ferry—again, a platform mounted on twin dugout canoes, poled by two skinny men across a river no more than seventy or eighty yards wide. Everywhere in India where there is such a ferry, a hamlet springs up—a few enterprising merchants put up huts which serve as stores and dwellings, selling bananas, fruit-flavored drinks, and the like. As soon as the village is established, a beggar appears. One hears a beggar's cry as soon as one's vehicle is within earshot; it persists until one has passed on.

At the second ferry, we heard the beggar's cry while we were waiting for the boat to take us across. It was the usual whine of the beggar, the nasal, husky moan: *"Aaanh! Aaanh!"*

At first we thought it came from a cripple lying in one of the thatched huts. We paid no attention until the noise drew nearer. Looking down, we saw it.

The beggar was a child—I could not decide if it was male

or female—of about four or five. It came struggling through the filthy dust. Its hands were off at the wrists; its feet were off just above the ankles. It was not born handless or footless. Scar tissue at its stumps made it plain that its members had been cut off. It continued its cawing cry, moving toward us, holding out its handless arms. Reinhold and I threw all the coins we had in our pockets. It smiled and threw itself onto the ground, picking the coins up with its lips. Lying there, it smiled again and cried out again.

As our car brought us into the village of Maramon, it was hard to believe that we were approaching a religious gathering. At convention time, the place is drowned in the tides of pilgrims that flow in from every side. They come from all over India, these people, bringing their own shops, roadside stands and shelters, throwing them up along the roads in such prolific confusion that no outsider ever can tell where Maramon itself begins and ends in the fifty-one weeks of the year when the convention is not in session. As many as 30,-000 people come to worship at the week-long services. But souvenir salesmen and snack vendors are not the only ones who come to do business with the crowds; there are also proprietors of hardware stores, dry-goods and notion shops, jewelers and craftsmen, and men who hawk clothing and sandals to replace those the worshipers have worn out on the journey. Pitchmen are everywhere, selling balloons, banners, rattles, clappers, and other noisemakers. In a huge lot on the Cochin side of the village, the government throws up an exhibition of Indian arts and crafts. Across the road, on a platform, two girls in purple and red saris do a dance as a barker promises more of the same inside. A daredevil rides a motorcycle at full speed around a dessert-dish-sized motor-drome.

Now we are here, and the sight of the convention itself is even more startling. We are on a cliff overlooking a dry river-bed. Below is a huge tent without sides. More than 20,000 people can sit under this huge canvas. With Walter Corlett, whom we have come to regard as our good friend, Reinhold and I go down the wooden steps to the riverbed to mingle with the crowds of white-robed pilgrims who are streaming to-ward the tent. Leading up to it is a kind of midway, with vendors on either side in smaller tents, offering books, re-ligious articles (pictures and mottoes, such as GOD IS LOVE, WHAT IS HOME WITHOUT A MOTHER? and VICTORY TO INDIA) and pamphlets. Nearly all the canvas stalls offer Bibles trans-lated into various dialects, plus books by and about Billy Gra-ham and other internationally known religious leaders and evangelists. There is also one stall labeled BEGGARS' RELIEF CENTER. We stop to chat with the people here. "So many beg-gars come, we have to put the almsgiving by pilgrims on a logical basis," the man in the booth says. "We try to put the beggars into classifications of Desirable and Undesirable. The former are those who really are Christians and really need to beg . . . the latter ones are those who pretend to be beggars just to get alms. We issue cards to the Desirables, and no pilgrim will give to a beggar unless the beggar has a card. Yesterday we issued over nine hundred cards."

The sun reflects off the brown-white riverbed sand into our eyes. We go into the tent, where Bob is preaching. As usual, his sermon is put in terms the people can see graphi-cally and therefore understand more readily.

The service lasts nearly two and a half hours—a remarkable tribute, it occurs to me, to the devotion and faith of these Indian Christians. I would be willing to swear that the heat, even under the tent, is at least 110 degrees and possibly more. It is too much for me. I go back up to the buildings on the cliff, where Dr. Paul Rees, a member of the World Vision pastors' conference staff, who has come to join Bob here, is working in his room. Dr. Rees left his home in Minneapolis on Christmas night to go to Australia to work with the team of Billy Graham, conducting one of Graham's famous crusades, then came up here, and after leaving will go on through Siam, Malaya, Indonesia, and other Far Eastern countries to arrange for the pastors' conferences. As soon as that trip is completed he will go on to Osaka to join Bob for the World Vision Crusade. Then he will go out on the pastors' conference circuit with Bob and the team. If he is fortunate, he will see his family again in mid-September. Already, this year, he has flown more than 50,000 miles; by the time the year is over, he will have covered nearly 200,000. He is in his mid-fifties; he is personable and gentle, a scholarly man who obviously would be more at home teaching theology in a seminary. Yet he, too, is driven on by the burden he has assumed. Again, as I have so many times on this trip, I begin to wonder what makes certain clergymen content to sit in their small, comfortable parsonages, writing their sermons, visiting their sick and aged, and what makes others reach out to those thousands who, living in ignorance and hopelessness, need the help of people equipped to give it to them. I look at Dr. Rees in his room. It is barren as a cell. Its walls are whitewashed mud. His bed is a few slats of wood laid over a frame, with thin matting atop them. There are not even nettings at the windows. He has only a chair and a table. As I stop in to greet him, he looks up from the sermon he is preparing and smiles, pleased to take a break; but as soon as we exchange a few words, he bows his head again, as though in prayer. Watching him, I realize that this man's entire life is a prayer. This is Paul Rees, minister of the gospel.

Bob comes up from the tent. Sweat is pouring off his face, and his shirt and trousers are soaked through. Still, he does not flinch when one of the ministers of the Mar Thoma Church comes up to him and asks him to go and see a hospital that needs help in putting up a new building. "It is not far off," the minister says. As it turns out, it is forty miles away, and the road that leads to it is a rough one. We pile into the car and go to see it: it is exactly the same as so many others we have seen this trip. The patients are crowded into small, dark rooms, the pharmacy has open shelves on which the drugs are kept, the operating room has a dirt floor. There is no question that the Christians here are doing a tremendous job under odds that would stagger people in the States. Bob promises to take up the need with his board, to see if he can raise some money for new construction.

We drive the forty miles back to Maramon. On the way, I remark on how astonishing it is to see so many Christians gathered in one place in India.

"Yes," Bob agrees, "there's nothing like this anywhere else in the Far East—and it's been going on for years and years. Some of the oldest Christian churches in India are in this section of the country. They gave up using one of their newer ones a few years ago—it was only eight hundred years old."

"We have many churches older than that," says the Mar Thoma minister. He is Bishop Athanasius, of Turavella. He wears a pink robe that drops to his feet, a black cap with a hood falling around his shoulders, and a gray-black beard. He speaks English with a distinct Oxford accent; later he tells us he was educated at Oxford.

As Bob and the Bishop converse, I learn to my surprise that this state, Kerala, turned Communist in the 1956 election. It is obviously a matter of grave concern to the local clergy. Although the Communists have not yet begun their usual program of religious persecution, they already have moved in on the schools sponsored by the church. The Bishop explains that formerly the schools paid their teachers directly. Now, under the Communists, the money must be paid into the state treasury, which then pays the teachers. This gives the state the power of deciding who will teach and what will be taught.

"Why did the state turn Communist?" I ask.

The Bishop hesitates. "It was dissatisfaction with the way things were going under the control of the Congress Party," he says. "Not long ago I met a local official who confessed to me that he had voted for the Communists, and I asked him why he had done so. He said, 'I did it for the same reason a man commits suicide—because anything would have been better than the existing conditions.' The Christian Church fought, but of course we are not strong."

We continue on our journey back to Maramon, but when we get there it develops that our day is not yet over. There is another hospital to see, and Bob agrees to go on the trip. By the time we go there, everyone is all but exhausted. Immediately after dinner, we go willingly back to our rooms. Lying there in the hot Indian blackness, trying to sort out my impressions of the day, I cannot help feeling relieved that this is the last stop of our long trip. In another day we will go back to Madras, then fly to Bombay and to Cairo, where Bob will leave us. In forty-eight hours he will be addressing a congregation in Park Street Congregational Church, in Boston, a date he agreed to take six months ago. . . .

For some reason, I awaken suddenly in the middle of the night. The luminous hands of my watch show that it is after three. There is a light in the next room. I turn over, trying to go back to sleep, but I am too hot, too keyed up. I decide that I will get up and read for a while, and go out into the room.

Bob is there, bent over a table, writing.

"I was having trouble sleeping," he says, "so I thought I might as well work. Whenever I get to the end of a long trip like this, I get sleepless. I don't know why, exactly—I suppose it's because I feel that there's still so much to do. Funny, isn't it? Here we are in this house, with beds to sleep in, and out there on that riverbed are thousands and thousands of people, some of whom came hundreds of miles to be at this convention, sleeping in the grass, sleeping on the ground. . . ." He shook his head.

"How did you happen to come to Mar Thoma in the first place?" I ask.

He scratches his head. "I've been coming here so long, I . . . wait, I remember. There was a young fellow who heard me preach once in Minneapolis, Joe Weatherly, who felt the call to go out to China. Before he could finish his education and go out there, China fell. He then decided to go to India, and our organization helped support his work. He did a splendid job. He had his headquarters in Bombay, but he preached all over the country—and he kept begging me to come down here and see the work the church is doing in South India. One time, on my way home from Formosa, I stopped to see Joe for a few days. He urged me to come down here and see some of the ancient churches, so we did come down and stayed in the home of one of the Mar Thoma bishops. While I was there they received word that one of the speakers for this convention wouldn't be able to come. They invited me. I've been invited back every year since, but I've only been able to make it about five times. It must have been about 1950 when I first started. We've helped them build some of the buildings at the Mar Thoma College, and we've helped out with some of the hospitals and clinics the church people have established. . . ." He stops. "Well, buddy, this is our last stop. Do you think you've got some material?"

I nod. "I've got the material. Pretty good sermon out there today, Bob."

"No," he said emphatically. "I preach lousy sermons. I'm not homiletical. But I thank God for the people I've seen come to Christ. You know, for the first two hundred years there weren't many churches. People just told each other the gospel, and what had happened to them through it. People just said, 'I don't know how it happened, but I met Jesus Christ and it made all the difference in the world to me.' I believe that. The only reason I can talk to people like those in that crowd today, like the icehouse people in Taegu, other people we've met on this trip, is that I'm willing to have Jesus put on the spot. I'm not afraid to have people put Him to the test to find if He is who He says He is—the Son of God.

"That's the reason every person we've met is in this work —because they all believe He is, and that He will do what He says He will do.

"I came to Jesus when I was a boy. He transformed my life. From then on I felt that I had something to live for and that He would do what He promised. I could put Him to the test. Jesus says He saves sinners. I believe it, for my life has all the potential for sin that any other man's has. Yet I go on praying that

He will help me keep from sinning and that I will be the instrument of what He wants me to do. I don't do these things He does them. I don't depend on schemes, foundations, big gifts to help these people. I depend on Him. I bank on His integrity. So do all the others you've met. We bank on the fact that if anything is breaking the heart of God, and we will do something about it, or if we are willing to do something, He will make it possible for us to do it. The mighty and the noble have the cleverness and the ability to do great things. We—the people you've met—aren't mighty or noble. All we've got is our God. He is enough."

Bob Pierce, sitting in the barren room, bows his head. He prays aloud, the same simple prayer I have heard so many times: "Let the things that break God's heart break mine."

POSTSCRIPT § OSAKA

It is now late May. Because I want to see for myself the results of the plans that were being made in Tokyo when we were there in February, I have come back to Japan to witness the final days of World Vision's Osaka Christian Crusade. And I have come back for something else. In the beginning, both in the States and during the course of my trip with Bob, it was difficult for me not to feel embarrassed by the men and women I heard reiterating their religious beliefs. Yet now, as I meet again the people I first met a few months ago, I feel an actual joy in the reunion. Little Sensei, bustling around welcoming people who have come to the Crusade; Bill Price,

Bob's traveling secretary, the calm and efficient minister whose deep faith is evident in his countenance; Ellsworth Culver, the second-in-command of World Vision, a brisk and boyish young man with a ready grin that conceals the essential seriousness of his nature; Larry Ward, of *World Vision Magazine*, a stocky, self-effacing man passionately dedicated to spreading the Word through his writings; these and many others. My joy in them comes as something of a surprise to me for I have met these people only two, three, or four times at the most. I know little about their personal lives. I know that Bill Price holds a pilot's license, I know Ellsworth Culver's mother because I met her while we were in Formosa, and I know Larry Ward's writings. Yet I don't know who is married and who isn't, where they live, how many children they have, or any of the things one ordinarily knows about one's friends. All I know is that they are united in their service, that they are inflexibly dedicated to their work, and that, oddly enough, I feel a kinship and a bond with them because of those things.

As soon as I check into the Osaka Grand Hotel, I feel a hand on my elbow.

"Dr. Gehman, I presume?"

Turning around, I confront the Reverend Mr. Dave Morken, the missionary-evangelist I met in Hong Kong. Dave has come to Osaka to spend a day or two with the Crusade Team before going off to set up arrangements for a Crusade he himself will conduct in Fukuoka, in the south. "We'll be going from September 16 to October 4," he says. "Of course, it won't be anything like the size of this meeting, but we're hoping the Lord will bless us. The meetings will be sponsored by the forty Protestant churches in the Fukuoka area, and we hope to draw people from the nineteen suburban areas around there as well as from the city, which has a population of about a million. We've got the sports arena booked—it seats seven thousand."

"How's the meeting going here?" I ask.

Larry Ward is nearby. "We're blessed," he says. "That is the only word for it. God is at work here. You have only to see the services to know that. During the first two weeks there were more than forty-four hundred decisions for Christ."

The Reverend Mr. R. S. Nicholson, a man I have not met before, who has been assisting Joe Gooden in the liaison with the Japanese, says, "Japan has never seen an invitation like this."

I find Bob in his room, lying on his bed. Even though he is exhausted, he jumps to his feet—and, again, I realize that I am back with a lifelong friend. It is as though physically meeting him has brought back, somehow, all the things we shared on that long trip. I can't remember when I have been so glad to see anyone. The only troubling factor is that he seems so weary. He has been driving himself again, and it is evident from his voice that he is all but exhausted. But his face carries its accustomed smile and I can see that he is pleased with the way things are going. "God really has blessed us," he says. "He's answered our prayers, and all those who've been praying. We've had over forty thousand people here already, and some nights we've been turning them away. The thing I'm happiest about is that so many of them are new people—those who have been here go home and tell others about it, and then they come. Also, our team has been going out every day to factories, schools, hospitals and other institutions. We've been reaching around two thousand a day that way. We're on the nationwide television and radio. It's wonderful—it exceeds all our expectations. I thank God every minute of the day."

Later, Douglas Cozart, Ellsworth Culver, Bill Price, and Larry Ward tell me some of the incidents that have occurred. A labor union official, who had been a professed atheist, came for several nights and, finally, stepped forward to accept Christ. He said to Gary Moore, one of the World Vision soloists, "I heard you sing in Japanese, and your heart spoke to mine. Then I saw you standing in tears during the invitation to come forward, and your attitude of love brought me to your Christ." A businessman's Crusade ticket disappeared. The next day one of his employees came to him and said, "I stole your ticket—I wanted to go to the Crusade, and didn't know how to get one. But I was saved at the meeting and want to know if you can get me six more tickets. I have friends who need to go." A headwaiter in the Osaka Grand Hotel went to one meeting, accepted the invitation, and went forward. Later, one of the ministers asked him how he felt. He said, "I feel that I have been turned inside out and upside down."

The stories go on and on, and I hear them on every side all the time I am at the Crusade. But to me the individual stories are not nearly as impressive as the services themselves. Osaka Festival Hall is the most modern, up-to-date concert hall in all of Japan. Its acoustics are perfect; its seats are situated so that each affords an unobstructed view of the stage, and they are more comfortable than those found in most halls in the United States. The first night, I go in with Sensei Webster-Smith; we arrive nearly forty-five minutes ahead of time, but the 4000-seat auditorium is already nearly filled. In the center of the stage's backdrop is a tall silver cross on a field of deep blue. In front of it on bleachers are the members of the five hundred-voice chorus, and on either side of the lectern are the members of the seventy-five-piece Kyoto Symphony. As the choir begins to sing, I am astonished by its sound. A stranger would not believe that this huge group has been assembled with only a few days' rehearsal. The people seem to have been singing together for years. The group has been put together by a member of the World Vision group named Ed Mills, and rehearsed by Ralph Carmichael, another volunteer.

The singers were recruited from the 25,000-odd Christians who belong to the four hundred or so chuches in the Osaka-Kyoto-Kobe section. Later, Ed Mills tells me, "The singers signed up for an average of five nights of service during the three weeks. We figured about a ten per cent no-show . . . but it's been much lower than that. Ralph Carmichael—he's done a lot of work on TV and radio in the States, with Desi and Lucy and other shows—arrived nine days ahead of the time the Crusade was to begin, and he conducted rehearsals twice in each of the areas from which the singers were recruited. Using an interpreter, of course, which added to his problems. We have them singing fourteen songs—some in English, some in Japanese, some in both. Each evening before the meeting begins, we rehearse the choir again. What really encourages us is that there are signs that this choir will stay together after the meetings are over, and perform at Easter and Christmas and on special Sundays throughout the year. There's a good chance of that—over three thousand people make up the pool from which the nightly five hundred are used. Everybody said it couldn't be done in three weeks, but we did it."

After the choir sings, the services follow the customary order of most Protestant ceremonies, except that there are more vocal selections—by Fague Springman, Gary Moore, Norman Nelson—and some instrumental numbers by Jack Conner (marimba) and Charles Magnuson (piano) and Lorin Whitney (organ). There are prayers, and then Bob preaches. As his voice sounds through the auditorium, I remember his sermons at the Mar Thoma convention, and how the immense crowd had listened without moving and without making a sound. This audience is much the same.

"They have been responding here," a missionary says to me, "because Dr. Pierce preaches a message of love. He not only faithfully preaches the message of God's redeeming love, he delivers it *in* love. The people sense his love for them, and they respond."

The sermon, like all of Bob's, is in terms the Japanese can understand. But he does not talk down, and he does not talk long. Finally he calls for the people to come forward.

They get up, hundreds of them, all over the immense auditorium. All sorts of people come up—a man who obviously is in business, a girl crying, an elderly man with a long, wispy beard, a young married couple. The atmosphere is one of dedicated reverence, as though these people have been deeply touched. It holds the entire audience in its grip, as the steady streams begin to flow toward the stage.

Sensei touches my arm. "Look over there to the left, near the middle." She is indicating a blind boy, making his way along with his cane ahead of him. Several of the people are on crutches. There are mothers carrying children, and people so old they must be supported as they walk.

"It's been this way every night," Sensei says. "I've prayed I would see it someday in Japan, and here it is. . . ."

After the meeting, in the lobby, I run into Joe Gooden, the man who was chiefly responsible for the meeting. "You ought to be feeling fine, Joe, at the success you're having here."

"We are, we are," he says. "But there's still much, much opposition, and there are other powerful organizations fighting us all the time. I read in the *Japan Times* the other day about the *Soka Gakkai*, which seems to be a kind of fringe Buddhist sect, about a million and a half strong. The *Times* writer described it as 'a religion of purgation.' Its political strength is apparently superior to that of the Communist Party. It's already got three seats in the upper house, and its strength appears to be increasing all the time. There'll be opposition to Christians from that group, mark my word."

Ellsworth Culver, of the World Vision staff, and I go to get something to eat at a tempura house near my hotel. "Well, Els, what's World Vision been doing since I saw you last?"

Culver passes a hand across his forehead. "What *haven't* we been doing?" he says. "Let's see . . . we've started sending funds to Lil and Dr. Barney in Formosa to begin constructing that hospital for mountain people at Pu-li. We've sent money for improvements on the Sun Nak Baby Home in Taegu, Korea—I believe you visited it with Bob on your trip. We bought a ten-passenger Landrover for the Haven of Hope Sanitarium in Hong Kong . . . that's the one Miss Annie Skau runs. Then we've started support for the St. Thomas Mission Hospital in Kottyam, South India. We've earmarked another twenty-five thousand for the Children's Hospital in Taegu—Dr. Moffett's hospital. Those are just new things, since we saw you last." He smiles. "Why didn't you do something to restrain Bob on that trip? He went around committing himself *everywhere*. He must have agreed to raise at least another hundred fifty thousand over and above our budget. . . ."

"Well," I say, "at least this Crusade will more than pay for itself, with the attendance you're getting. The offerings ought to help."

Culver laughs. "The offerings here aren't even a wet spot in the bucket, let alone a drop. The collection amounts to less than thirty dollars . . . and we've got TV time to buy, and radio, and newspaper advertisements, and the meetings in the schools and factories and prisons and hospitals, and the staff to feed and house, and pastors to bring here from all parts of Japan. . . ."

"I thought these events usually made money," I say.

"If you put on a big crusade in a United States city, you *might* make your expenses," Culver says. "But in the Far East, it's impossible. You must just depend on raising the whole amount, and know you're not going to get a penny back. These people have very little money, don't forget. Moreover, we've got a considerable body of expenses to meet after we leave here. We're going to keep an office open for eight months, with a staff to supervise the activities of the volunteer counselors. You see, once a person has come forward, we don't want to lose him. So we send counselors to meet with the new people, and try to get them into local churches. After Bob leaves here there'll be rallies in Kyoto, Kobe, and Osaka—efforts to keep the people in the church. And on July 3, Bob will come back for one day to address the new Christians and anybody else who wants to come. . . ."

We say good night and I go to bed, again reflecting with something akin to awe upon the dedication of the World Vision people. Culver and I have talked until nearly one; at 7 A.M. there will be a prayer meeting in which Bob and his lieutenants will make plans for the day. Strangely enough, I find myself looking forward to the meeting. . . .

Dr. Paul Rees is here, I find as we assemble in the morning. We reminisce for a moment about our meeting in India. He has been traveling continuously for six months; after the Crusade is over he will be off on a round of pastors' conferences. Yet he is as vigorous and enthusiastic, in his reserved way, as he was when I saw him in late February.

After the meeting, Paul suggests that I go to a luncheon meeting being conducted by William C. Jones. This is a name I have not heard previously.

"He's a remarkable fellow," Paul says. "He's got quite a story to tell—and he's telling it all over the world. Every year he travels nearly two hundred thousand miles, from continent to continent, holding meetings for business and professional leaders. He pays for the meetings himself."

I learn that Jones has scheduled eight such meetings in Osaka and in the Kyoto-Kobe area. More than 1600 influential citizens will attend them. On the day I go, there are nearly four hundred gathered around banquet tables on the top floor of Festival Hall. Since Jones is a businessman, the affair is conducted in a businesslike manner. It opens with a prayer, a minister says a few words, and the men settle down to their lunches. Then the minister stands again and introduces Bill Jones.

President of a printing company in Los Angeles, Jones indicates at once that he is not a man to waste words. He speaks bluntly, without particular emotion, and for that reason his story is all the more dramatic.

"Six years ago," he says, "I was successful in every way—except in my life. I had a business that all but ran itself . . . except that I was neglecting it, and it was falling apart. So was my marriage. I was—and still am—married to a wonderful woman. We lived in a big and expensive house and we had everything we could have wanted. Except happiness. For no real reason that I know, I drank constantly—morning, noon and night. I was an alcoholic. My wife and I were on the brink of divorce."

Then, he continues, he asked Jesus to come into his heart. He does not say who led him to Christ; he simply makes the statement.

"The taste for liquor left, never to return. My wife and I fell in love again, and were as happy as we were when we first met. And my business began to flourish again. Something else occurred to me. I did not need all the money I was earning. I realized that money can be important only if it is invested in the means for telling others what Christ has done for one sinner."

He urges his listeners to do as he has done.

Glancing around the hall, I notice three or four men leaving. A few are listening with unconcealed boredom on their faces, showing plainly that they do not believe what Jones is saying. But, for the most part, the audience is rapt—and not, I realize, because it is exhibiting the traditional politeness. The people are paying attention because they are looking for something. As I am, I think a bit later. I dismiss the thought at once.

Jones concludes the meeting by urging the luncheon guests to attempt to find Christ as he did.

The meetings go on and on for the next few days—in schools, hospitals, in a prison, before industrial groups. I go along to some, and am continually astonished by the response to the sermons and hymns. The time flies. I do not see much of Bob; he is far too busy, for he is preaching in the daytime sessions as well as the night ones, and I don't feel that I should disturb him.

It is on my last morning that it bursts upon me—the thing that has been growing in my subconscious. I go to the 7 A.M. prayer meeting, but do not get a chance to talk to Bob—he is listening to reports, making suggestions, conferring with his fellow ministers and the constant flow of Japanese pastors who come in just to shake his hand. In the middle of all this, I feel something take hold of me. That is the only way I can describe it. It would be false of me to describe it as a true mystical experience; it is, instead, a kind of illumination in which everything suddenly snaps not into focus, precisely, but into awareness. It makes me nervous, and yet it is calming. I deny it, but there is no denying it. It is as true and real as my palms, sweating with emotion, and it is only with enormous effort that I keep from opening my mouth and telling about it. Friends who have known me for a long time will scoff at this. I can only report that it happened. I get up. I rush back to my room. There is only one thing to do. I sit down at my machine and begin to type:

Dear Bob,

This morning in the prayer meeting I found, to my utter astonishment, that I wanted to say a prayer so badly that my entire body was shaking, but I held off because I am not as well equipped to express myself orally as the rest of you and also because what I wanted to say was too personal. At the moment it happened I automatically doubted it, but I now know as clearly as I know that my fingers are striking these keys that it is true. If I had spoken—and I should have—I would have said, "Lord, I came to this cause of Christ as something of a skeptic as well as a stranger. Except for my small technical ability to interpret events for mass audiences, I was hardly qualified or worthy. But through the instrument of the ministry of Dr. Pierce, and through what I observed of the people I met, I sit here now not as an alien but as a friend and, more meaningful perhaps, a believer. I pray that Bob may be given the wisdom and strength to carry on, and that his co-workers and friends be given the zeal and endurance to go on healing the sick, comforting the dying, clothing and feeding the destitute, and bringing to all the message of Christ and His principles. Finally, I pray that I may be given the strength and the toughness, the illumination and the understanding, to spread the word of this work among the ignorant and unbelieving so that all may know some measure of the glory of God." That is what I would have said—but I said it inside myself.

Folding the letter is like attacking it, so swiftly and vehemently is it done, and I tuck it into an envelope with a frantic haste, as though some small part of my old self might take control and cause the new part, floundering and pliant as a newborn child, to expire. I scramble up the stairs to Bob's room, which is just above mine, fasten the note in the clip on the door, and rush back to my own. I pack, frenziedly. I do not know, exactly, what to make of what has happened, and I do not want to think about it, not now. This has nothing to do with reason or rationality. I know that eventually it will have everything to do with it, which is why I must not tamper with it at present.

By noon, packed and ready to leave, I call Bob to say good-by. He is not in his room.

"He's gone to speak at a luncheon meeting for businessmen," Bill Price tells me.

I get my bags downstairs, check out of the hotel, and go a block away for a final taste of tempura. As I get back to the hotel, I see that the driver who is to take me to the airport is already there waiting. They load in my bags. Then—at the last minute—Bob arrives. He comes up and we shake hands.

"When will I see you again?" I ask.

"Well," he says, "from here we go to Australia—I have a

couple of meetings to speak to down there. In two weeks I come back here. Then I go home for a couple of days, and we start out again for the pastors' conferences in Malaya, Singapore, Thailand, and the Philippines. Then I'm going to try and get a couple of weeks with my family at the end of the summer before I go back to India and Indonesia. When I return to the States I'll have a speaking tour. Maybe we can get together then. On the second of January of next year we start out on another tour. Come, let's have a word of prayer." There in the lobby, he bows his head and prays. He grabs one of my shoulders and shakes it.

"God bless you," he says.

"God bless you." It is the first time I have ever said this phrase with sincerity. And as I say it, I realize that these people's belief in Christ has changed my life. Something has happened to me which, as yet, I am unable to define or evaluate. But it has happened. It is tangible—almost as tangible as the flight bag over my shoulder, the reporter's burden. The word *burden* makes me think of my new friends, and what I have learned from them, and how they literally have led me. I want to do something that will tell them what has happened to me, and then I realize that that is unnecessary. They know. All along, they knew it would happen.

Bob Pierce punches my shoulder, then waves his hand. He is off again.

ABOUT THE AUTHOR

A prolific contributor to national magazines, as well as a writer of books, Richard Gehman was born thirty-nine years ago in Lancaster, Pennsylvania. With his wife, Betsy, and his young daughter he lives in Carmel, New York. In 1960 he taught at the writers' conferences at Indiana University and Bread Loaf, Vermont.

ABOUT THE PHOTOGRAPHER

A prize-winning newspaper photographer whose work has often appeared in national magazines, Richard Reinhold lives in Lancaster, Pennsylvania, where he and Richard Gehman grew up together. He is married, and the father of two daughters.